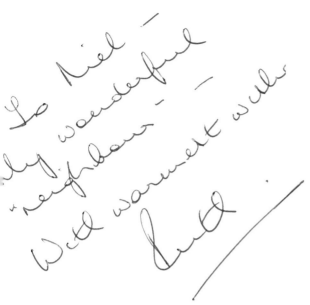

To Niel —
my wonderful —
neighbour —
With warmest will

A LIFE IN MUSIC

RUTH NYE AND THE ARRAU HERITAGE

by

Roma Randles

Grosvenor House
Publishing Limited

This book is published by
Grosvenor House Publishing Ltd
28-30 High Street, Guildford, Surrey, GU1 3EL.
www.grosvenorhousepublishing.co.uk

A CIP record for this book
is available from the British Library

ISBN 978-1-78148-553-8

To Ruthie With Love

"The most blessed and privileged of all callings is that of the musician, who acts as interpreter, inspirer, teacher, healer, consoler and above all, as a humble servant..."

Yehudi Menuhin

CLAUDIO ARRAU

To Whom It May Concern ḷ

RUTH NYE was a student of mine since 1960,
and has developed into an artist of unusually
high standards.
Her superb musicianship, her great artistry, her
technical skill, and her innate sense of style
have secured her success on the concert-stage,
whereever she appeared.
The young devoted artist is outstanding and
undoubtedly belongs to the very best of the younger
generation of pianists.
Any promotion she possibly could get would be
higly deserved.

Signed:

Claudio Arrau

202 Shore Road
Douglaston L.I., New York,
N.Y.

CLAUDIO ARRAU

Claudio Arrau was born in Chillán, Chile, on February 6th 1903. His father died when he was two years old. He gave his first recital at the age of five.

In 1911, the Chilean Government gave total financial support for the prodigy and his family (mother, aunt, brother, and sister) to move to Berlin, so that the young Claudio would be given the best possible opportunity to develop his extraordinary talent.

He fortunately was introduced to the distinguished pedagogue Martin Krause, by the Chilean pianist, Rosita Renard. Krause had studied with Liszt in Weimar, during the last years of the Master's life.

This is an important aspect of this book:

Claudio Arrau studied with
Martin Krause, who studied with
Franz Liszt, who studied with
Carl Czerny, who studied with
Ludwig van Beethoven, who studied with
Joseph Haydn.

Ruth Nye studied with Claudio Arrau and is therefore an important part of this long unbroken musical chain.

Arrau became a prolific and tireless performer. In all one reads about this great artist, one claim stands alone...he was considered to have been one of the very few remaining links to the great musical traditions of the last century, and for more than half a century he was one of the world's most respected and sublime interpreters of Beethoven, Schumann, Chopin, Brahms and Liszt.

Daniel Barenboim said that he was always astonished by the manner in which Arrau joined the nineteenth and twentieth centuries, creating the best of both worlds. "The music was really in his blood, in his bones, and his utter integrity and stamina are incredible." He also spoke about his particular sound...he felt it had two aspects. Firstly a thickness, full-bodied and orchestral when he wanted that, and secondly an utterly disembodied amazing timbre...quite spell-binding. Daniel was always supremely grateful for the way Arrau had staunchly supported him from the start, and that their friendship was such that they could intelligently argue points of difference over an evening together.

Sir Colin Davis spoke of Arrau's total considerateness to performers and to new conductors. "His sound is amazing, and it is entirely his own...no one else has it exactly that way. His devotion to Liszt is extraordinary. He ennobles that music in a way no one else in the world can." Sir Colin recalled many

occasions when they collaborated and found their collaborations utterly mutually satisfying. "When you do something really good together, this wonderful maestro utterly delights in the shared experience. He has great humility as well as musical greatness." Finally the gravely composed conversationalist, Sir Colin Davis, said emotionally, "Arrau gave me what I lacked as a child...that warmth and closeness I needed. I was utterly devoted to him."

In 1937 Claudio Arrau married Ruth Schneider and there were three children: Carmen, Mario and Christopher.

He died in Mürzzuschlag, Austria, in 1991 and is buried in his birthplace of Chillán, Chile.

FOREWORD

Ruth Nye is a highly sensitive and discerning musician who is spiritually far more advanced than most. She possesses great musical integrity, and her musical philosophy is profound, wide-ranging, and refreshingly individual. She possesses impeccable musical taste, and following her musical association with that supreme master, Claudio Arrau, she has inherited his granite-like sense of structure and dynamism, thus expanding music through limitless realms.

She is well aware of the dimensions that great music can and should reveal, and her astonishing imagination, warmth and depth (as well as humour) are all hallmarks possessed by the rare soul blessed with true enlightenment.

In a world where inverted standards and dubious musical fashions abound, she has helped countless individuals see the true purpose of music, thanks to her innate authority, and profound realisation of the powers of this great art.

JOHN LILL
November, 2008

John Lill came to international attention when he won the coveted Tchaikovsky Competition in Moscow in 1970. Known for his aristocratic interpretations of Beethoven and the great masters of the nineteenth and twentieth century piano repertoire, John Lill performs all over the world and was awarded a CBE in the 2005 New Year's Honours List.

INTRODUCTION

I can say without hesitation, that Ruth Nye totally changed my life and my approach to the piano and to music in general.

I have gradually found myself insisting that the story of this remarkable but totally unassuming woman simply must be put down. It is a story that must be told.

Unlikely though it may seem, this extremely busy woman now in her mid-seventies cannot see anything very remarkable about her life. She does not see herself as being unique. She took a great deal of persuading to become involved, but once she did, it was with her usual enthusiasm.

Though Ruth was not overly keen about any type of 'biography', my own feeling is that in order to pay her the respect that is her due, it is absolutely necessary to look at her early life and those events that helped shape **Ruth Nye MBE, FRCM.**

Ruth did have one emphatic thing to say and that was, "Never mind so much about *my* life, my biography as it were. What is much more important is to write about the *legacy* I was given through my years of study and association with Claudio Arrau, and the heritage I am therefore able to pass on to my students. It is my students I am more concerned about..."

AS IT HAPPENED

It was August 1999, and eighteen of us were gathered in the superb drawing room of the private residence of the Australian Embassy in Paris. High above the city, this large formal reception-room with its walls of glass on three sides gives a spectacular 270-degree outlook over the winding River Seine, its bridges, and almost the entire spread of one of the world's loveliest cities.

We were there as guests of the Australian Ambassador. When the Ambassador, John Spender, heard that we were looking for a venue for a lecture/recital from the concert pianist Ruth Nye, he readily issued an invitation to use their private residence.

Ruth is small in stature, with her still light brown, thick hair tied back in a loose chignon, a serene face and manner, and a charming melodious voice which is perhaps, after more than forty years of English life, overwhelmingly English in accent, though not entirely so. Above all, it is musical, gentle and arresting for her listeners. Her brown eyes are especially warm and penetrating, yet can sparkle with fun and humour, and her laugh is distinctive.

Ruth gave a talk on Chopin's life, from his birth until he settled as a young man in Paris, and played relevant compositions, beginning with a very youthful Polonaise and finishing with several Etudes. Her delivery as always was disarmingly low-key and charming whilst at the same time, I was very aware that it was also absolutely factual, with enough analytical comment to satisfy those who were more knowledgeable, and with anecdotes and details to engage the group as a whole. One sensed the attentiveness, appreciation and total engagement of all.

Several Embassy staff members had joined the group to listen to the lecture/recital during this Chopin Anniversary Year of 1999. Her playing was beautiful, and I was struck as always by Ruth's particular demeanour at the piano, head slightly to the side in an attitude of listening, a posture perhaps of empathy for the music and the composer's intentions, but also a special awareness of the character of the instrument itself. One was also made aware of the strength she could evoke from those small white hands when the music demanded it through her relaxed but powerful arms, the range of the dynamics she produced, and the overall beauty of the quality of her sound.

In 1999, I was conducting my eleventh annual European Music and Art tour for small groups of Australian music lovers. Ruth Nye joined us for five or six days on several of these journeys, giving lecture/recitals in many different locations, and speaking on a variety of musical topics.

These tours have covered many different parts of Europe from Russia, Scandinavia to Sicily. Art experts are engaged to conduct the groups through the major galleries, and history lecturers bring the cities we visit alive for the participants. In 1999, the tour was titled **"Anniversaries and More"**. Incredibly this was a year of several very notable anniversaries, including those of Frédéric Chopin (the 150th anniversary of his death), Johann Goethe (250th birthday) and of Friederich Schiller (140th birthday). A very special concert was given in a state-of-the-art stadium erected in the beautiful countryside between Weimar and Buchenwald, and where a combined Israel Philharmonic and the Bayerische State Orchestra played together...the very first combination of German and Jewish musical forces since the war. It was an unforgettable experience.

Elsewhere in Weimar, the next day Daniel Barenboim was rehearsing a very new young orchestra of Jewish, Palestinian and Arab musicians, the 'West-East Divan' which, despite initial difficulties, is still together and proof of the power of faith in overcoming difference. The West-East Divan is actually a humanitarian idea of both Barenboim and the late Edward Said, and Daniel Barenboim describes it as being "...a forum where young people from Israel, Palestine and the Arab countries can express themselves freely".

Remarkably that year, 1999, also celebrated the 80th birthday of the Weimar Republic, the 80th birthday of the famous Bauhaus School, the 10th anniversary of the fall of the Berlin Wall, and the 100th anniversary of the death of Johann Strauss II. Our tour that year had been constructed so as to visit the locations and to participate in the celebrations of them all; a momentous year indeed.

In some wonderful venues and locations, Ruth has delivered her well-researched, beautifully presented and often immensely moving lecture/recitals on different composers and their music. Outstanding ones were her Eduard Grieg in the Concert Hall built next to his home in Norway, where the rake of the seating area enabled the audience to enjoy not only the music but also the dramatic view of the fjord. At this recital I was delighted to join her at the piano for a 'four hands' performance of the Peer Gynt Suite.

Her late Liszt in the Conservatoire in Oslo was wonderful and reduced several of her audience to tears; magical Debussy in Nice, (Ruth has a special way with Debussy's colours); Schumann in Dresden, which was extraordinarily moving; and Mendelssohn in Leipzig. In so many locations, including St Petersburg where she played and talked about composers who had lived for a time there, all the talks were totally engaging and captivating for our different and most appreciative audiences.

Ruth always interacts fully with the different groups, participating in lively conversations over meals in often spectacular locations, joining the excursions we take, and sharing her gentle wit, wisdom, anecdotes and hilarity on occasions too. She is always much appreciated.

....

My original connection with Ruth Nye dates back to a shared experience of having studied with the renowned Australian teacher, Lindsay Biggins. When I was a first year Bachelor of Music student in Melbourne, Ruth was already a star, winning everything and performing widely. All I did was admire from afar, but I did follow her career when I had the time and opportunity.

Then in 1979 we came back to England with Jacqueline and Justin, our two youngest children, who were to spend two years at English schools. Young violinist and horse-mad Jackie had had several lessons at Ross Nye's stables in Hyde Park. These stables were in narrow cobbled-stoned Bathurst Mews, very close to the park and a stone's throw from Paddington Station. Above the stables was the Nyes' London flat, and it was here that Ruth saw a very few students as she was still very busy in her performing life. Sometimes I used to sit in the car waiting for Jackie and could hear the music emanating from the floor above and occasionally chatted with Ruth. On impulse one day, and with great trepidation, I asked if I might come and play for her. She agreed, and I began to revise a suitable work from my repertoire. I was overjoyed but also extremely nervous about the prospect.

She was inspiring, a wonderful teacher for someone of my age, education and experience (I think I was forty-three). She taught me aspects of technique I had never known. She led me to think about interpretation in a way I had not previously considered; she allowed nothing to slip by. Always so observant, she had ideas on phrasing I had not visited; she would suggest a change of fingering for some passage, which would result in it being a little less circumspect and therefore creating more colour, and she pushed me into works which hitherto I felt I could not possibly tackle but now could, simply because I was practising in a new and previously unimagined manner. She advised me regarding so many finer points of teaching. We discussed art and literature, we shared laughter; she told me stories of her life in music but it was quite a time before I heard much about her long association with the great Claudio Arrau and how he had taught and inspired her. Ruth is a modest person, and these facts emerged only very gradually, though of course I had known a certain amount before I went to her. I lived for those weekly sessions in Bathurst Mews. They were taken very seriously indeed. I practised religiously for long hours, using methods Ruth had suggested. I sometimes practised with closed eyes, often very slowly...closed eyes and a deep slow penetrative feeling of the notes. "Enjoy it," she would say, encouraging a truly sensuous approach during this particular method of practising. But this was only one of many new technical and interpretive approaches. She opened my eyes to so much, and it was not till some time later that I realised I was *relearning* how to play the piano, relearning it the Arrau/Nye way. I was also becoming more demanding of myself and often became quite nervous, feeling that what I had prepared was not going to be up to scratch. The joy was that, if in fact it was not, she found ways for me to see clearly how it *could* be right next time...and it would be.

I remember that after each session with Ruth, I would drive into nearby Hyde Park and stop close to the Serpentine where I could see the water and could contemplate what we had covered and what had newly inspired me.

Chopin Ballades and Etudes, Bach "Italian Concerto", Granados "The Lover and the Nightingale", some Debussy Preludes, Liszt "Sposalizio"...these and many more were addressed in different ways, and required much devoted work and study. When the time came all too soon to return to Australia I missed her and our sessions together as we had become such friends.

My subsequent visits to Ruth and Ross Nye were always very enjoyable ones, and I always felt so at home staying with them at Longfrey, their country home in the green valleys of Surrey. Longfrey Farm was also a Riding Holiday venue, the "Family Business" one could say.

LONGFREY FARM

The property has a most interesting history, associated with, of all things, gunpowder!

The manufacture of gunpowder really had its origins in what is now Germany. It was introduced into England during the reign of Elizabeth I, and was produced at several sites where the timber most satisfactory for charcoal was readily available. These were notably the Lake District, Essex and Surrey. As technology developed more sophisticated explosives, the number of factories was reduced. With the invention of cordite, all production went across to this, and black gunpowder became a thing of the past.

Interestingly, the great English essayist, William Cobbett, who was born in Surrey and rode through the English country side with the intention of producing his collection of essays "Rural Rides", wrote of the particular beauty and variety of the Vale of Chilworth, "but the gunpowder factory goaded me to fury".

When the Chilworth Gunpowder Production Company was in full production in the mid-nineteenth century , a complex of units was built on the property for the foreman plus three workers and their families. This is actually the original five-gabled building of the Longfrey house. The foreman claimed two of the central units, so that he and his family would be somewhat insulated from the icy winters. In the early 1900s the then foreman had a small family. One, a daughter born in 1910, actually came to meet the Nyes when they bought the property in January 1977. They continued to have occasional telephone conversations with her until she died, having requesting that her ashes be scattered on the Longfrey property, which indeed they were.

The mills were a major source of munitions during the Great War. In 1919, after Versailles, the company closed down and the property was sold on the open market. The first owner bought it in 1924 and began to incorporate all the separate units into one house...as it is today. The Nyes are the fourth owners of Longfrey Farm.

It is a unique five-gabled three-storey residence, with its elegant drawing room which houses the two magnificent grand pianos, a Steinway, and Ruth's pride and joy, a Fazioli. This sunny room is lined with bookshelves and mementoes of all kinds, some framed photos of musical celebrities, including a delightful one of Claudio Arrau relaxing in a hammock, under which is written, **"To my dear friend and outstanding pupil, Ruth Nye, with all affection and warmest wishes for a very successful future."**

To my dear friend and outstanding pupil Ruth Nye with all affection and warmest wishes for a very successful future
Claudio Arrau
Amsterdam 1964.

There are comfortable chairs, a large fireplace, and graceful windows looking out over the lake and its majestic swans and rambling gardens. It is obviously the combination of two rooms, and of course, is a salon, which breathes music. The kitchen is large and old fashioned but, with its stunning new cooker and plentiful large dressers and cupboards, works wonderfully. These days, two large and beloved dogs at certain times of the day set up rather an effective obstacle-course to be negotiated before one can even get into that kitchen, which is quite disconcerting at times. They are Bryn, a cross between a golden retriever and a collie, and Holly, a rescued yellow Labrador, who are much loved and honoured members of the Nye Family. There are numerous pantries and storerooms, a separate comfortable and more casual sitting room with huge fireplace, a dining room large enough to seat twenty people, and how many bedrooms and bathrooms is hard to estimate...a lot! The second floor is the main bedroom floor, the third only being used when the house is absolutely full. It is a wonderful family home, which has welcomed hundreds of visitors from all over the world, including many at the top of their musical careers.

Longfrey Farm is quite large, some sixty acres, through which a small stream runs, and is approached via a rough unsealed track and surrounded by woods and rolling hills. The track itself can become troublesome in bad weather. It is not until one turns in through the Longfrey gates that the going is any easier. The grounds are far from manicured but there is a definite beauty there, much varied wildlife and at the rear of the house really lovely terraces of blooms reach upwards.

On one particular visit I looked out from my bedroom over a scene of such serenity. Some horses were grazing in green fields, the river bubbled past, and on the glassy lake with its

island in the centre, a male swan was keeping a wary eye on some ducks, water hens and colourful pheasants, which he would chase very aggressively if they dared to enter, or be near, the water. The object of his unwavering concern was his mate who was huddled over the recently laid eggs on the nest they had built at the edge of the island, and it was there she must remain for five long weeks until the cygnets hatched. At different times of the day I looked in vain for some signs of movement from her and marvelled at her quiet dedication. The lake changes depending on the time of the day. At about 6pm it resembles a mirror, reflecting the blue sky with its few fluffy clouds and the trees nearby.

During riding holidays, there can be up to fifteen children, plus assistants to deal with the twenty-five horses. The incredible thing is that this pianist and sought-after teacher does all the cooking for these large groups; usually using produce she herself has grown in her large, well-tended vegetable gardens. All through the year she cooks and freezes so there are always ready meals for unexpected guests and gargantuan ones for these riding groups, which she herself serves in the dining room. Ruth puts it quite simply: "I like to think this keeps my life balanced and I enjoy doing it. Also when I pursued a busy concert career, it was my husband, Ross, who supported me for so long and now I wish to support him. We are in this together." This is said with such finality and dignity it ends any possible argument to the contrary. Here is the real Ruth…a total woman, in every sense of that word, entirely lacking that certain 'preciousness' of some career musicians. Grandchildren, cooking, growing, caring, advising, are all bound up with her teaching at such an advanced level. Her energy and ability seem boundless, as is also her joy in so much of it.

Visiting Longfrey so many times, and watching and listening to all that goes on during Riding Holidays is an experience in itself. I have heard Oxford University educated daughter Kirsty, who is a highly skilled and qualified horsewoman and who now runs the Ross Nye Stables, talking to these young people about Greek Tragedies and Mythology and other literary and historical matters. There is a lot of laughter, and real care and warmth towards the young riders who are sometimes far from their homes and families, coming from all parts of the world.

Of course, there is one part of this large house the young people must not invade, and that is the drawing room, which is where Ruth practises herself and sees her already actively performing young concert artists. Over many years I have so often been privileged to sit in on these inspiring lessons with her brilliant and responsive students. Many times I have stared out of the windows at the water with its ducks and swans and felt moved almost to tears as they played.

IT WAS MEANT TO BE!

The story of Ruth Nye began in Brisbane, Australia, some 793 km north of Sydney and 1,425 km from Melbourne. Brisbane is close to the Pacific Ocean and beautifully situated on the Brisbane River. It is an attractive city with humid subtropical climate, though these days it is becoming more and more congested. Non-convict European settlement here commenced in 1838 and Queensland was proclaimed a separate colony in 1859 with Brisbane as its capital. The City of Greater Brisbane was not formed until 1925, and was governed by the Brisbane City Council, which also became responsible for the encouragement of its young talent, for which we must be thankful. In the forties, it encouraged the highly talented Ronald Farren-Price and his younger sister, Ruth, both extremely gifted pianists. Though the city at the time was quite provincial compared to both Sydney and Melbourne much further

south, it was an excellent place for these two remarkable young musicians because they had the very good fortune to be offered regular Radio Australia broadcasts and recitals in the City Hall and elsewhere. They had therefore very quickly become accustomed to public performance and a certain notoriety because of it. But Ruth says, "We didn't think we were anything special. We were so used to it, we just did it. As a child, when you are very good at something, it is always fun, never a hardship or unduly challenging at any time. And our lives were quite normal in all other respects."

They played solo works, duets together, and two-piano works...later on, also concertos with the Queensland Symphony Orchestra.

These children and their younger sister (who is also musical and artistic) Beverley, were the three children of Ruth and Leslie Farren-Price, who lived in the leafy suburb of Ascot, Brisbane. Leslie Farren-Price was a businessman, who built up a highly respected watch and jewellery business.

Ronald, two years older than Ruth, was a brilliant young pianist, and little Ruth, listening to him practise, would try to pick out the notes of his works on the piano and begged to be taught to play as well. She commenced formal lessons at the age of six. Ruth tells a story of how for the first time, when she was thirteen, she fully realised how important playing the piano had become for her. She had been playing at lunchtime in the school grounds on a climbing frame...jumping up and catching the bars, when she fell heavily to the ground, badly injuring her right arm.

Sitting in the staff room while her parents were contacted, she nursed her obviously seriously injured arm, and found herself whispering in alarm to herself, "I'll never be able to play again! I'll never be able to play again!" It was only at that point, she recalls, that she realised how precious piano-playing had become to her.

The Farren-Prices were advised that Brisbane was too small a musical environment, so Ronald, being the elder, was sent to

Melbourne to study with the highly regarded Lindsay Biggins. This teacher, who had studied at the Leipzig Conservatory, and also in Paris, was considered to be the best piano teacher in Australia during this period. One year later Ruth was sent as a weekly boarder to the Methodist Ladies' College, where the general education was excellent. She too then began studies with Lindsay Biggins.

Ruth enjoyed her time as a weekly boarder at MLC where the musical involvements were exceptional. There were choir, madrigal groups, music appreciation classes, chamber music and orchestra as well as a glee club. Ruth has always loved singing and has always considered it an essential part of musical training. (Claudio Arrau later told her you couldn't play anything well on the piano if you couldn't sing it, and she continues to reinforce this idea.) The principal, acknowledging her enormous talent, permitted her to commence her Diploma of Music course because she had been awarded a scholarship to the University Conservatorium, while she was still in her final year at school. This was quite an extraordinary move. But academe as well as music presented no problems for highly intelligent and able young Ruth...she took it all in her stride and gained very high results, topping her year at university. Meanwhile the entire Farren-Price family had now moved from Brisbane to Melbourne, so the family were all together again and stability restored. There were two pianos at opposite ends of the house for individual uninterrupted practice by the two gifted young musicians.

Melbourne society at the time was often fairly stuffy. There was a certain smug, self-satisfied suburbanism in many quarters. Nonetheless, for those of us interested in education, music, theatre and culture generally, the early fifties was a wonderfully invigorating time.

The city today is so totally different, a smart, vibrant, modern and above all, cosmopolitan city in every sense of the word, where all the arts are first class.

It was in this cultural climate that both Ronald and Ruth Farren-Price were launched on their respective careers.

I never knew the Farren-Price parents, but they must have been rather good-looking because all three of their children were very beautiful. All the girls were in love with the dashing, handsome Ronald, and Ruth, quite apart from her brilliance, was blessed with beauty, a captivating smile and a sparkling, laughing personality, enormous assets for any striving newcomer to the concert platform. Younger sister Beverley, also very musical and who had also studied with Lindsay Biggins but had chosen not to go down the same career path, was also very beautiful...today, in fact, the most glamorous of the three. Beverley now says, "Ruth was beautiful, glamorous and a star even in those early days. She also had a personality that attracted everyone like bees to a honey pot."

....

Ruth always praises the musical opportunities available in Australia at the time. She broadcast the Mozart 'Coronation' concerto live on the ABC radio at the age of twelve and continued to broadcast (again live) regularly on the prestigious *Young Australia Series*. At fourteen she played Beethoven's First Concerto in the Brisbane City Hall. In 1952 she won the Victorian State Final of the ABC Concerto Competition playing Kabelevsky's Second Concerto.

....

In the early 1950s Ronald, now studying in London, attended a recital by Claudio Arrau and was so overwhelmed that he went backstage to introduce himself. Arrau suggested that Ronald come to the Savoy Hotel the very next day. Arrau was very impressed with this young pianist and worked with him when he could on his visits to London. It was Ronald who introduced Ruth to Arrau in 1954 when she joined him in London. She remains extremely grateful to him for this. Arrau told Ronald and Ruth that his greatly admired friend, Rafael de Silva, was going to be in

Stuttgart for the summer and suggested they study privately with him, which they did for four months. Rafael de Silva was a very good pianist but seriously crippling pre-concert nerves had prevented him from making a successful career as a performer. Arrau and he had been students at the same time in Germany, and Arrau had always been extremely impressed by his musicianship and ability and saddened by the fact that his incapacitating nerves had prevented a well-deserved international career. He was, however, a really wonderful teacher and Arrau completely trusted him as his deputy, knowing he would teach exactly what he himself wanted. Rafael de Silva believed totally in Arrau's approach to piano playing and had a remarkable understanding of the means of achieving the right qualities of sounds called for.

....

Financial circumstances meant that Ruth had to return to Australia at the end of 1954. Back in Melbourne, after a recording session of some Chopin Etudes for the ABC radio, Ruth was lunching with Lindsay Biggins when he collapsed; he died in hospital that night. It must have been the most harrowing experience for Ruth. They had been very close, and she owed him so much.

His death impacted greatly on the musical life of Melbourne and left his teaching post at the Conservatorium vacant. In discussions with the Ormond Professor, Sir Bernard Heinze, Ruth suggested that the post be offered to her brother. Sir Bernard was delighted with the idea, and Ruth deputised for Ronald until his return some time later in 1955; he proved to be an inspiring and most sought-after piano teacher.

....

Ronald Farren-Price AM, was awarded the Order of Australia for Services to Music in 1991, and was the recipient of the Dublin prize in 2002. More recently the University of Melbourne conferred on him the honorary degree of Doctor of Music, and in this he is only the sixteenth recipient in 150 years. He has performed in the major concert halls of many countries, including twelve visits to Russia.

He says...

"*My first memories of the piano are associated with Ruthie. From our early days as pianists, apart from our solo works, we played four-hands and two-piano works as part of our basic repertoire.*

"*Perhaps our careers in this form of ensemble culminated in performing the Mozart Two-Piano Concerto in E flat, K 365, as soloists with the Melbourne Symphony Orchestra when we were both in our thirties. At the time we both wondered, 'How often have a brother and sister played this concerto professionally since Wolfgang and Nannerl played it originally in Vienna?' Our conclusion was "'Probably not very often!'"*

As youngsters, Ruthie with her slight figure and dancing brown eyes and Ronnie in short trousers would enter all the local Brisbane and Queensland Eisteddfods, mostly winning from the 'Twelve years and under' to the 'Open' sections".

Ron remembers, "*We began to feel sorry about actually winning, thinking how the other competitors had to cope with sinking hearts as they saw us approaching!*" Such proximity for two siblings in working together could have created either friction or a great bond. Clearly the latter was the result.

"*Our days in Brisbane as children were happy overall for the three of us. Certainly our father maintained a strict regime in most aspects of life and his strong work ethic was passed on to us all. Nevertheless, in retrospect, we are grateful for this and happily in combination with our mother's gracious elegance, the parental vigour and drive were well balanced.*

"*Our teacher in Brisbane, from our first lesson, was Edna Hosking. She was a family friend and an excellent teacher who gave us a sound start. It must be remembered that in the 1930s and 40s there was no Conservatorium in Brisbane.*

"*During 1946 I was heard by Hepzibah Menuhin, who strongly encouraged me to go to Melbourne with her friend Lindsay Biggins.*

"*I was accepted by Lindsay Biggins and commenced serious study in 1947. Just after my arrival I was selected to play the First Movement of the Grieg Concerto with the MSO in the Concerto Finals (no winners were chosen in those earlier years). Our parents arrived in Melbourne for the Melbourne Town Hall concert. The previous night they had listened to Ruthie playing the First Movement of the Beethoven C Major Concerto in the Brisbane City Hall. Almost immediately arrangements were made for Ruth to become a weekly boarder at M.L.C. so that she also could study with Lindsay Biggins. Of course, Lindsay was captivated by her vivacious talent and personality.*

"*Our parents decided to uproot from Brisbane and settle in Melbourne, where our father opened a branch of his watch business. Of course, this was a major change in life style for the whole family. The youngest sibling, Beverley, was also enrolled at M.L.C., and Lindsay Biggins taught the three of us. It would be true to say that we three enjoyed our close companionship...they were wonderful years.*"

....

On holiday in Queensland in 1956, Ruth met the dashing Ross Nye, who had spent the past several years with his brother on their property in the Far North Queensland Outback. They fell madly in love. Ross's love of music was a significant factor, as Ruth later says: "He was tall, bronzed, had muscular shoulders...a magnificent specimen of a man. And he loved music!" They married on the 7th of November 1956.

She and Ross spent their first year as newly-weds living in Brisbane, where Ruth performed a lot. It was during this time that she again played to Claudio Arrau who was on tour for the ABC. Following the advice offered by Arrau, Ross decided that they should move to Melbourne because there were more opportunities for her there. Both daughters were born in Melbourne, Kirsten in 1958 and Lisa in 1960.

In 1959 another career commenced compatibly in conjunction with her performing. During these early days of Australian television she was interviewed to publicise her recital programmed for viewing on Mothers' Day, which led to her being offered a temporary position as a presenter for the ABC. However, the audiences liked her so much she was asked to stay on.

There she was, not only a well-known pianist, but now a television personality as well! Ruth announced what was coming up, just chatting, and also interviewing people. She never received any training...she was just a natural performer, had a lovely voice,

and was never afraid of speaking. In those days of reels and tapes, something often broke and the necessary splicing took time. Ruth, who would perhaps have been practising in another studio, would be called in urgently to fill the gap, which she always did with aplomb. Management had also worked out a system of pre-recorded short performances of hers for such emergencies.

The presenter of the *The Music Room*, a half- hour programme of live classical performances, retired and Ruth took over that as well. She, with international and local artists, would perform classical works and talk about them to her viewing audience.

She gave the very first live televised concerto performance in Australia, playing the Schumann Concerto.

Ruth was awarded a 'Logie'
for best Television Personality in 1960.
Presented by the American television star Hugh O'Brien.

Arrau toured Australia again in 1962, and after one of his recitals he said he was interested to hear her play again. He and his wife lunched at the Nyes' home and after the meal they spent time at the piano. Among what she played for him that day was the Debussy "L'Isle Joyeuse". He was impressed, obviously finding some very special quality in her playing and it was then that he strongly suggested she should come to New York to study with him.

Arrau was to perform in Tasmania and suggested Ruth fly over to work with him further. It was in Hobart that Ruth Arrau was extremely encouraging and invited the Nyes to stay with them in Douglaston, until they found a place of their own in New York.

In 1963 the Nye family left for New York and were never to return to Australia for more than visits. They flew from Melbourne on a very hot January mid-summer's day, and landed in New York. As they approached the airport, they could see icicles hanging from the bridges. Ruth Arrau met them at the airport and looked after them wonderfully. Arrau was away on tour at the time and Ruth recalls how they had a really lovely time staying with Ruth Arrau, *"who was a most marvellous and dependable woman."* With Ruth Arrau's help they rented a small apartment in Bayside not far from the Arraus' on Long Island Sound.

Whenever he was away on tour he gave Ruth the freedom to practise in his superb studio rather than on the small upright they had rented.

The day before their tickets expired the family flew to London where they knew Ruth would be able to continue working with Arrau, as he visited frequently. It also gave them the opportunity to experience life and music in Europe. They rented a cottage in Surrey near Guildford.

Ruth's English concert career began to develop and then snowballed. They had been advised, "You won't get anything for at least two years because all agencies have full books." However, the concert-going public loved her, and in less than a year she had performed in the London Pianoforte Series at the Wigmore Hall.

By now they had decided they very much liked the English way of life and the English people. Ross looked around for a suitable stable to purchase where he could start a riding school. He found a fairly run-down stable in Somers Mews, Central London. This seemed the ideal opportunity to allow Ruth to be in a major musical centre and to give Ross his own business working with horses. They knew from the start that there were plans to redevelop the Mews, but it gave them a starting point so they signed the lease for a year, which was extended to five years while redevelopment plans were finalised.

Sally Mellor, who had studied with Ronald Farren-Price in Melbourne before marrying and moving to England, writes about her visits to Somers Mews:

I visited Somers Mews...an old stable on the north side of Hyde Park. It was impossible to keep wisps of straw off the stairs but the riding boots were always stacked neatly on the bottom step. One climbed those stairs usually to the sound of some wonderful Chopin or Liszt coming from Ruth's and Ross's bedroom. Their bed had to be folded away each morning in order for anyone to sit down and play the piano.

Ruth's concert schedule, by this time, was considerable both in the UK and in Europe. Her workload was immense but she agreed to take me as a pupil on the condition that I worked very hard.

Her teaching was about giving one the courage to be different so long as it was musical and one did not cheat...ever! Difficulties are there to be solved, not facilitated. The very tension created by the difficulty gives the expression.

Soon Ross, Ruth and family moved to Bathurst Mews where there was more space, and the lessons continued, but now on a grand piano above proper stables with that delicious mixed smell of horses and leather.

I was fortunate to attend the series of remarkable Master Classes given by Claudio Arrau in Bonn (to mark the bicentennial of Beethoven's birth), in which Ruth participated. Ruth was chosen to play in the final concert, which was broadcast over German radio.

My last memory of Arrau was at a tea party organised by Ruthie. When I asked him about why he hadn't recorded Haydn, Arrau replied, 'That is for my old age.' He was then in his eighties!

....

In 1970 Somers Mews was finally demolished and they and the horses were rehoused in the much larger stables, in Bathurst Mews, with a three-bedroom flat above.

Family photo from a magazine article
about Ruth taken in Somers Mews

After about twelve months Ruth was performing regularly in London and abroad. There was never any discussion about returning to live in Australia, though of course, Ruth toured there professionally and once they took the girls for a holiday. The girls were happy and doing well at their schools. In addition, they had access to their ponies and the nearby enormous park. They were meeting interesting and lovely people in both the riding and music areas, and their lives were becoming increasingly satisfying. England had become their home.

Kirsty Anthony, the Nyes' elder daughter, shared some early memories with me.

She was four-years-old when the family went to New York, and even at that tender age, she remembers feeling somehow it might be a risk for them. She recalls encountering colour television for the first time, "Wow!" and meeting some lovely people who were supportive of them in the rather difficult life they had undertaken.

Daddy paid $300 for an old Lincoln Continental in which we went on trips, including up to Vermont to stay with the Arraus.

We used to be taken to the Arraus' home in Douglaston where Lisa and I played with Chrissie (Christopher Arrau), who was between our ages, when my mother practised or had lessons there.

Uncle Claudio was always kind and gentle...he told me I had a pianist's hand...and he and Aunt Ruth were an old-fashioned, aristocratic kind of couple, with beautiful manners.

Kirsty remembers also a wonderful trip in the Lincoln Continental for a Christmas in Mexico. This was turned into an educational trip, as they had to sing appropriate songs passing through each state and were told much information about each of them. Because of Ross's lifelong interest in bloodstock, *en route* they visited horse studs including those of the Kentucky thoroughbreds.

When they arrived in London, she remembers seeing Churchill's funeral on television while they were staying for a while with Vi Cockrell, a very dear friend, in St John's Wood.

Vi was a very British, no nonsense lady, and a wonderful support to us.

We then rented 'Lord's Hill House' in Shamley Green, Surrey. The owner only wanted to rent it out for a few months but we managed to get it for a year. I turned five. I was tiny and thin, and always much younger than the others in my class, but I did well academically.

Our lives were fitted around Mummy's career, but symbiotically her career centred around us. There was never any money to spare for things like baby-sitting, for example. Lisa and I were always taken with her, both to rehearsals and to performances. We didn't know that what she did was very special…we just went, and we behaved very well for long periods of time, which seems a bit remarkable to think about. I even remember turning the pages of the Cesar Franck Violin and Piano Sonata for Mummy when I was thirteen or fourteen (maybe younger), while it was being recorded. That was by no means the only time either.

Kirsty is so appreciative of the way her parents brought them up. Although she was, of course, conscious of not having things other children may have had, she was aware that such material issues were unimportant.

There was no money then but it was all managed so intelligently, and we had everything we needed but no luxuries whatsoever. Mummy used to be a bit aghast when people gave us expensive inappropriate gifts and she would say, 'Such a waste of money…why didn't they think of books?' And books, reading, reading, reading is what was always encouraged for us (as well as much outdoor life). This is why we eventually did so well academically, I am sure.

Lisa Goldsworthy, second daughter, works as a consultant emergency paediatrician at the Bristol Children's Hospital. She shared some early childhood memories:

I remember Mummy practising for many hours a day and needing an afternoon rest, often with her Siamese cat, Genghis Khan; Daddy's desk covered with publicity fliers he was sending out prior to her performances, especially the Queen Elizabeth Hall recitals; finding Romford library and other performance halls (we would often travel all together with Mummy to different places: even Milton Keynes with its many roundabouts) – some venues were more of a challenge to find than the South Bank or Wigmore Hall; phone calls from Ibbs and Tillet; bouquets of beautiful flowers in the bath after a performance. Mummy always looked fabulous for her performances, often in dresses she had made herself that gave her enough ability to move freely when playing. She also supported master classes that Rafael de Silva ran. My childhood memory of him is of his unusual after-shave, though this might not do justice to his prowess as a musician!

The Mews flat would be visited by other musicians coming to practise with her: we became familiar with different violin and cello works as a result, as well as some unusual personalities! Sometimes there would be a big party after a musical event, and Kirsty and I would help with taking coats, passing around food.

Importantly, my parents have always supported each other. Mummy made the mounted fancy dress costumes for the annual London Horse Show and did all the cooking and preparing for the children staying for riding holidays. Daddy was always there for her and for her music. There was a strong network of friends too: especially Dee Barr and Vi Cockrell in those early times.

When Uncle Claudio came to London, she would virtually drop everything to spend time with him. My parents would share happy times with him: trips to The Savoy, where he always stayed in London; late dinners after his performances. I remember a favourite restaurant in Connaught Street, 'La Lupa' and the manager, Luciano: sometimes even Kirsty and I would be part of the group. Claudio Arrau was a very special person in my parents' lives.

....

In 1974 Ruth was asked by the Australian High Commissioner to chair a committee for a Royal Gala Variety Show to support the 'Help for the People of Darwin' appeal. Ann Ball, who had first become friends with Ruth and Ross from the early days of the Riding School when it was in Somers Mews, recalls these events:

The terrible Cyclone Tracy had devastated the city of Darwin, and we were aiming to raise money for this large project. It was the most amazing six weeks. We put together a wonderful show at the Prince of Wales Theatre, hosted by Danny La Rue, on February 9th 1974.

After the successful gala, Ross asked me if I would consider taking on the role of Ruth's PA to look after the arrangements that had to be made when she was touring. I agreed with alacrity and spent the next four years touring with her.

In 1977, I organised a series of recitals for her in the United States. One of the more memorable locations was a winery in California where the case of the beautiful Steinway, that had been lent for the recital, was somewhat unusual. It was 'powder blue' to match the 'blue rinse' colour of the owner's hair!

I was thrilled to be able to arrange our journey home on the QE2, in exchange for Ruth performing two short recitals. It was a perfect ending to the tour.

I look back on those four years with much joy and friendship.

Elizabeth (Liz) Barwell is Head of Keyboard at Melbourne Girls' Grammar School. Liz had studied with Ruth as a child in Melbourne.

London, 1975 – end of 1980:

The Nyes: What a combo! The piano upstairs in Bathurst Mews...Ruthie practising for yet another Queen Elizabeth Hall concert and below, sixteen much loved horses for the Riding School.

I completed my B. Mus. degree at the University of Melbourne and then life took me to London. Once there I hoped that Ruth would have time to work with me. Luckily she agreed and I was given the education of a lifetime. I also met the most famous pianists of the time who would often practise at the Mews. I recall sneaking up the stairs to listen to Richter or Arrau practising!

Ruthie adored a party, both giving them and going to them, and was always the centre of attention with her beauty, her love of people and her delicious sense of humour. Her own Ross is the centre of her universe and I recall my mother asking Ruth, "What is it that inspires you to such excellence and loving giving in all that you try to do?" Ruth answered swiftly and simply, "Ross!"

Ruth included students in her life...allowed us to soak up this world of the artist...to immerse ourselves.

Ruth calls every day a spectacular adventure and instils this passion and love for humankind in all she does. I haven't seen Ruth in over fifteen years now but she lives within me and in my teaching every day.

During this time Liz was very grateful to Ruth and Ross for the monthly workshops they organised in Australia House, for the Australian Music Association, where young musicians had the opportunity to perform and receive criticism. It was through the Australian Music Society that Ruth became friends with the celebrated Australian pianist Eileen Joyce.

Eileen Joyce, born in a mining town in Tasmania, became an internationally famed concert pianist.

I remember introducing myself to this great artist when she was one of the adjudicators at the Sydney International Piano Competition at the Opera House in the 1980s. I said I was a great friend of Ruth Nye, and was told delightedly, "Oh, Ruth! She does wonderful work. In fact I would say she is one of the very best piano teachers in England."

Interestingly, when young, Eileen Joyce and Lindsay Biggins had once studied together at the Leipzig Conservatory, and

Lindsay Biggins always made much of her during her visits to Melbourne.

In the late 1970s and early 1980s Ruth performed not only in the USA and UK but in Australia, the Far East, the Middle East and throughout Europe. Some notable highlights were four performances of Beethoven concertos Nos 1 and 3 with Sir Malcolm Sargent, both books of the Debussy Preludes at the Queen Elizabeth Hall (one of six recitals there), and in the same hall the premier performance of Malcolm Williamson's third concerto, with the composer himself in the audience. Emmy Tillett extended her London Pianoforte Series to include Ruth's Wigmore Hall debut and also at Wigmore Hall the first performance of the then newly discovered piano transcription of Beethoven's String Trio in Eb major Op3. The work, having been authenticated by eminent musicologists, was originally offered to Claudio Arrau to give the first performance. However, as his schedule was already full he asked Ruth if she would do it.

With Ann Ball's administrative assistance the career was buoyant and seemed set to continue indefinitely. However now, on the way to the airport each time, Ruth began to think, "Why am I doing this to myself?" Of course, when she arrived at the destinations and met welcoming and interesting people who fêted her, the excitement would return. She enjoyed the actual performing but the loneliness of hotel rooms and the reality of the travelling and being away from her family, the doubts would again creep in. She and Ross discussed this many times and in the 1980s came to the decision that Ruth would, as she puts it, 'step off the international circuit' and only accept UK dates. No sooner had this happened, than the phone rang and someone in Germany was on the other end asking her to come to play the Grieg Concerto. "Oh, the Grieg, (which she adored performing)...marvellous, yes indeed!" But hang on she thought...you have just made a very big decision. She asked this entrepreneur to give her the telephone number and she would call back. Over dinner she and Ross discussed it all again...and they decided, Grieg or no Grieg, the answer would have to be a "No". She must remain firm. It took a lot of guts actually to make that decision after so many years.

When I asked if she had missed it, she thought for a while before answering,

"Well, I missed the excitement of it all, performing the major works, the adulation and being entertained so wonderfully. But all at such a price...being away from Ross and home so much, and that awful, exhausting travel, which no sooner had one arrived home, seemed to start all over again. And I was sick to death of living out of suit cases!"

The girls by now were no longer little girls, of course. Kirsty had read Law at Oxford, and Lisa was now a Doctor.

....

A SIGN FROM ABOVE?

It was in the early 90s that the fifth finger on Ruth's left hand became afflicted by a condition called 'Dupuytrens contracture', which caused her little finger to gradually curl into the palm of her hand. The implications for a concert pianist can only be imagined. This condition, which affects the palmar fascia, causes the fibrous tissue to shorten and thicken, resulting in total loss of flexibility It was named after the French surgeon, Baron Dupuytrens, who, in the 18th century, first demonstrated a surgical procedure to treat the condition. However, results were very limited and the condition usually returned.

The condition gradually worsened until finally she had surgery under a noted surgeon. In Ruth's words:

"This was a bit of a farce, because the after-care was practically non-existent and I ended up not even able to play an octave." Ruth said at the time, "I wondered if this was some kind of sign from above, because it pushed me totally into teaching."

This was a very important and significant point in the life of Ruth Nye. She continued to play but, as she said to me,

"It is now with a restricted repertoire because of the limited stretch, and a lot depends on the actual shape of the chords. Very often, even though I continue to do it, playing is quite physically painful for me now."

....

A TRIBUTE FROM PIERS LANE

Piers Lane's playing career has taken him to more than forty countries. Though born in London, he grew up in Brisbane, like Ruth. He is known internationally as a recording artist, recitalist, and concerto soloist with major orchestras and conductors. He has written and presented over 100 programmes for BBC Radio 3, was a professor at the Royal Academy of Music for twenty years and is the Artistic Director of the Australian Festival of Chamber Music.

When I picture Ruth in my mind's eye, I see her dressed un-fussily, her pretty, peachy face upturned, hair pulled back in a girlish ponytail, eyes twinkling with warmth and welcome, thoughtful enquiry, a merry seriousness...and a touching humility that betokens a person who, though she has achieved so much during her hard-working life, still takes nothing for granted.

Ruthie's presence has gently underpinned my professional and personal life in England the past three decades. She was never one of my major teachers, but has had a great influence on me nonetheless. She has always been generously encouraging and has frequently proffered practical support. It was partly her nod which convinced Arrau's former manager, Georgina Ivor, to undertake my own career management. She's sat for days turning pages for me at recording sessions, sharing my grumpiness with producers' demands! Once she had to beat a hasty retreat from a final session to welcome a new grandchild into the world. At odd times when I've been at an emotional low before an important public performance, she has been there to help...has had me to Longfrey and made calm observations of my playing, spurring my imagination or refocusing diffused thoughts just at the right time. And after that musical nourishment, there's likely been a seafood casserole to follow, with home grown veggies and lots of wine and a comfy bed for the night, with a healing breath of Surrey country air to complete the refuelling recipe. And always Ross there too, with his Queensland directness, wry humour and sunny outlook. 'Happy Days!' is the Nye toast at dinners, and days are inevitably happy when spent with Ruth and Ross. Their values are old-fashioned and centre around family and home, animals and garden, and behaving responsibly and inclusively. And educating students of all ages, of course, whether it be in piano-playing, horse-riding, dog-training, how to set the table or how to dry the dishes.

The Nyes are givers. I have yet to see Ruth take a real holiday to recharge her own batteries. She's one of those rare creatures who manage to attain contentment and balance through constant hard work and interaction with others. She retains a youthful gusto and enthusiasm for the things she's always done, and maintains a seemingly calm outlook and good order in her life. Of course this is aided by her supportive partnership with Ross. Their long marriage is an inspiringly real one.

Ruth has a great and deep understanding of music. I suspect performance itself was not really her natural habitat...she wasn't a 'stage beast' reaching her greatest playing heights in front of a huge audience. Ruth of course did lots of important concerts in her time, enjoyed by diverse listeners, but she was born to be a teacher and mentor. I've coached her students at the Menuhin School and have shared students with her at the Royal Academy of Music. I've watched her many times bring gifted children to a certain musical maturity by their late teens and early twenties. I am always thrilled to observe how they metamorphose into musical idealists, probing musicians, always looking for meaning.

Ruthie is regarded as an Arrau disciple, spreading his gospel. But that is only part of the story. She may impart his approach to technique and tone production, musical shaping and thought, but she's also great at observing her students' innate personalities and keyboard possibilities, developing their individual talents purposefully. There is always more love to give, more insight to encourage and I think she finds it difficult at times to 'let go' of her students. Students are treated as bona fide *members of the Nye household for years on end.*

I've probably made her sound an awful 'do-gooder'. She does do good, all the time; but she remains natural and uncomplicated. She likes, and gives, a good hug, happily sharing a bottle of wine and news of friends. Her friends sometimes despair that she doesn't take more time out for herself. But she's possessed of an unusual degree of dedication to her chosen roles and an untiring love of things musical and people-centred; and I can quite imagine her carrying on for eternity in the same way she has outstandingly carried on ever since I've known her.

....

THE YEHUDI MENUHIN SCHOOL

The Menuhin School, although famed for its teaching of stringed instruments, always had a small number of piano students. The appointment of an artist of the stature of Nikolai Demidenko to the teaching staff was intended to raise the profile of the piano department to that of the strings. In 1992 a second teacher became necessary and Demidenko suggested that Ruth was the person with whom he would most like to work. Demidenko knew Ruth through his agent Georgina Ivor, who worked closely with Arrau when she was at Harold Holt, Arrau's UK management.

The school itself is beautifully situated not far from the village of Stoke d'Abernon in Surrey, surrounded by wonderful rolling countryside.

Yehudi Menuhin founded the school in 1963 to provide musically gifted children from all over the world with the opportunity to study with the best possible teachers in a supportive and creative atmosphere. From the time of its foundation until his death in 1999, Menuhin devoted much time and thought to the musical development of the students. His wish was to create a microcosm of world society where differences of any kind would be unimportant. This philosophy succeeded more than he could ever have realised at the beginning. The students are selected irrespective of financial background, race or creed. It is now recognised as a Centre for Excellence in the Performing Arts, and is supported by Government as well as by patronage. Although students are selected for their musical abilities, there is an emphasis on academic excellence and the school comes high in national results. 97% of the graduates take up careers in the music profession.

Lord Menuhin is buried at the base of a tree that he had planted in 1996 to celebrate his eightieth birthday. He remains close to his beloved children and they to him.

Important artists visit to inspire the students by performing and giving master classes; this is a significant part of the school life.

Sport is important, but is limited to those kinds of sport, which are not too rough or inclined towards possible injury. Long, fast, cross-country walks; swimming and various ball games are compulsory. Ruth is delighted to note that skipping is now included.

Ruth currently shares the piano teaching responsibilities with Marcel Baudet.

The Menuhin School – Old Stable building

From Malcolm Singer, the Director of Music:

"Ruth Nye has been teaching at the Yehudi Menuhin School for twenty years. I have been working with her for the past fourteen years and we have become very good friends as well as very supportive colleagues.

Ruth is undoubtedly one of the great piano teachers in London. Her pupils are utterly devoted to her, and her colleagues both at the Yehudi Menuhin School and in the profession generally, admire and respect her enormously. Ruth's great teaching stems from her great humanity. Her teaching adopts an holistic approach – dealing with the whole person, and not just how they move their fingers at the keyboard. She aims to gently 'civilise' her students, to help them understand and internalise the music they are performing. This requires them to develop a true sense of scholarship, so that they find out when a work was written, why it was composed, for whom it was written, for what kind of instrument it was written; then to know about the composer's life, and the state of world affairs at the time.

Of course, the students may well have their own ideas as to how a work should be interpreted, and Ruth would never dream of squashing their creativity. However, for her, quite rightly, the text is paramount, and she will gently point out to a student if she thinks they are deviating too far from the composer's intentions. She will also guide them in matters of stage presence and presentation. She is certainly not expecting rigid formality from them, but a certain sense of decorum and the ability to communicate in a confident and relaxed manner with the audience.

None of this should suggest that Ruth is not rigorous about technique. Quality of sound at the keyboard and the means of obtaining that sound are vital to her. General issues of arm-weight are at the top of her agenda and once students learn to relax and control their arm weight, they usually find that they have the ability to draw an infinite variety of timbres from the keyboard. Ruth's 'technique classes' are often as much about mental dexterity as finger exercises. Scales and studies play an important role in these classes but are never taught in a dry or sterile fashion. The students are encouraged to devise more and more complicated ways of delivering scales…not just thirds and sixths, but seconds, fifths and sevenths; not just traditional contrary motions, but beginning on different notes and at different times, and with each hand moving at different speeds! All of this is done both with conventional and unconventional fingerings and rhythms. With arpeggios, different inversions may be played in each hand and many devious and inventive mental teasers are often introduced. All these 'games' serve to keep the students' brains awake, make them learn the geography of the keyboard at the same time as developing strength in the fingers. Of course all exercises can be tackled with different forms of articulation. If all this sounds tortuous – it is! However, it is delivered with such a joie de vivre, with such a sense of creative adventure and with such a feeling of gentle caring, that students not only respond to the challenges, but positively enjoy these stimulating classes.

Each February, Ruth and I take a group of young musicians on a short tour of Scotland with a concert in Edinburgh, and two for the music society at Blair Atholl. Ruth's ethos and profound beliefs permeate these events. The students are not only expected to play wonderfully (which they invariably do), but also to interact with the concert organisers and then with the audience at post-concert receptions. She creates these situations to help them develop many other skills that a concert artist needs off the platform as well as on it.

In the summer, Ruth and Ross open their home to all our piano students for a concert for a small select audience. This is always followed by a sumptuous barbecue. Once again, students are expected to pull their weight in ways other than just performing. They are expected to help clear away the plates and do the washing up, which inevitably ends in laughter! Ruth creates such a glorious ambience that even the grumpiest of teenagers relishes being part of the occasion and suddenly becomes a responsible and caring young adult. This is what I mean about the 'civilising' *approach to her work. This is all achieved with the minimum of fuss and no sense of self-congratulation. Indeed, the students are often transformed without really being aware of it happening...the sign of a great teacher!*

Although no longer a young lady, Ruth is perhaps in the prime of her teaching career. Her colleagues and her pupils all hope that she will continue with the same energy and dedication for many years to come.

....

From Bobby Chen
I commenced studying with Ruth Nye at the age of twelve at the Yehudi Menuhin School, and what a journey this turned out to be! She would dedicate herself to her students, always inspiring them...It was incredible to learn that she had spent time with the Chilean maestro, Claudio Arrau, and she told us all about Arrau's time under Martin Krause, a pupil of Franz Liszt.

Ruth always emphasised the importance of reading widely and listening widely. She encouraged all her students to attend live performances and to read the composers' lives as well as a wide range of good literature. She would always ask us to voice our musical thoughts and express our musical ideas and aspirations during the lessons. Her aim, she said, would be to enable her pupils to teach themselves.

During term time there was always the Thursday morning 'Technique Class'. Ruth would always be fresh and alert at 8am, but some of us had just started to crawl out of bed or from breakfast. Remarkably Ruth would remain unperturbed. There was not an occasion when she would raise her voice, even when some of the playing would make another professor throw the score out of the window. This elegant grace of hers would carry over into general dealings with people.

Her dedication to her pupils would mean that in preparation for important performances she would spend extra time teaching us in her home, Longfrey Farm, or at her piano studio in the Mews in London. What a privilege it was that she was willing to spend so much of her time with us. Ruth is still working extremely hard. Some of her friends have suggested she may like to think of slowing down a bit, but for Ruth this seems to have gone unheeded.

She would also help with the much needed exposure for her students. I will never forget the many performances she arranged for me directly or indirectly as well as taking me to see possible sponsors. Many of these have borne fruit with the concerts and sponsorships helping me through some difficult years. I shall remain very grateful for this always.

At the end of any occasion at Longfrey Farm…a recital, a birthday celebration, a party or a barbecue, who could ever forget their phrase, "Happy Days!" always said with such good cheer in their voices?

I congratulate Ruth on her many successes as a performer and as a teacher, and her just recently having received the MBE from Her Majesty, Queen Elizabeth the Second, as well as being elected a Fellow of the London Royal College of Music. She deserves all this and so much more. Lastly, but not least, who could forget her husband of more than fifty years, Ross, who is just the most wonderful person in his own right? Ruth always said that her career would not have been possible without his support.

I am extremely privileged to know them both."

....

Bobby Chen, a past student, has gone on to perform widely. One of Bobby's many CDs was described by a London music critic as being from "an armour-clad player of complete technique, a thinking musician and a natural romantic. His Schubert positively glows, his boldly projected Haydn impresses for the Michelangeli-like clarity of execution. His Petrushka, a marvel of exacting detail and precision attack, triumphs with the best…a powerfully coloured, authentically Russian journey."

THE MENUHIN HALL

2006 saw the realisation of a dream, when the superb new concert hall at the Yehudi Menuhin School opened. Mstislav Rostropovich, the great cellist (who became President of the school after Menuhin's death), spoke of his delight that a fitting memorial for his late great friend was now a reality.

Yehudi Menuhin was created a Life Peer in 1993, electing to be known simply as Lord Menuhin of Stoke d'Abernon,

"The most blessed and privileged of all callings is that of the musician, who teaches, and who acts as an interpreter, inspirer, teacher, healer, consoler, and above all, as a humble servant. These are the human roles I would endeavour to cultivate among my beloved group of students who enrich my school not only with

their burgeoning talents, but also with the great diversity of their cultural backgrounds."

The occasion was celebrated, as Menuhin would have wished, by a memorable concert given by the students. The school orchestra opened the programme with composer/music-director, Malcolm Singer's tribute to the occasion, 'Opening Rites', for which he positioned all the string players round the balconies of this wonderful soaring hall, and included a performance by two of Ruth's students of Ravel's 'Valse' on the hall's two new concert grands...a magnificent Steinway and a glorious Fazioli; Paolo Fazioli himself came from Italy for the occasion.

The event concluded with a champagne reception.

GENTLE PERSUASION

Terry Lewis, who is a close family friend and frequently accompanies Ruth on music tours, began to study with her during his time as the buyer for the Piano Department at Harrods. During his tenure it fell to him to organise the centenary celebrations for the department, 1894-1994. The highlight of the celebrations was a 'press breakfast' which, as the name implies, is a breakfast for the press, but given it is Harrods it meant the serious press, not your local paper. Ruth often tells her students that a pianist must be ready to perform at any time, so this was put to the test and he asked her to give a recital at 8am!

Representatives from Classic FM, the broadsheets and top end music magazines all attended. Ruth spoke briefly about the works she would perform, Mozart, Schubert, Liszt and Debussy. After the performance Terry was approached by an elegant, but rather ancient lady, who told him she had only come along because she had been at one of Ruth's Queen Elizabeth Hall recitals and couldn't believe her luck that she would get to hear her again. Oh, and she finished the conversation off with the minor point that she had once been a student of Rachmaninov!

When Terry moved to Jaques Samuel Pianos in 1996 he organised a series of lecture-recitals in the shop at Marble Arch. One such event Ruth gave on Schumann's Kreisleriana. Sometime later he asked her to present a talk entitled 'My Time With Arrau'. Ruth resisted for years but after much gentle persuasion from Terry she finally agreed.

The lecture took place on February 6th 2005. The audience included many professors of piano, young pianists and piano teachers. It was scheduled to last one and a half hours but was extended to over two hours. At the request of the audience a second more in depth lecture took place one year later.

The following is a summary:

MY TIME WITH
ARRAU LECTURE ONE

February 6th, 2005

Ruth commences her lecture:

Arrau was born in Chillán, south of Santiago, on February 6th, 1903. He died in Austria on June 9th, 1991.

Arrau's father, Carlos Arrau, was an ophthalmologist, whose ancestors, with the name of Arrhurt, were French provincials, who settled in Barcelona. One Arrau, an engineer, was sent by the Spanish King to Chile and his reward for services rendered there was a large amount of land near Chillán. There was some ancestry also from Scotland about which Arrau was quietly delighted. A son was Carlos...he was very kind to poor patients, it is said, but not so kind to his wife...a womaniser, with many illegitimate children. Claudio even knew one of them. Claudio was barely two years old when his father died after a horse-riding accident, so he never really remembered him.

His mother, Lucretia, was from a good Spanish family and a gifted pianist. She was forty-three when Claudio was born, having been married for twenty-one years. She died in 1987, only four weeks short of turning a hundred years old. In her later years, Claudio and Ruth Arrau took her to live with them in Douglaston, New York. Claudio was actually playing the Brahms D minor when she died and he always thought of her when playing the slow movement of that concerto.

There were many debts after Carlos died, and all the land was sold to clear these debts, so his mother commenced teaching the piano to support her family of three children. While she taught, two-year-old Claudio listened to the students and when they couldn't get something right, so the story goes, he would climb on the piano stool and play it correctly. He lived on that piano stool, he said. "I was often spoon fed on that stool." He could play music before he could read words. "Those black dots were no mystery to me." Never taught, he instinctively understood. "I was born playing the piano. I slipped into this world playing the Mephisto Waltz. I was in love with it."

His mother played the Mendelssohn Rondo Capriccioso very well. The little boy lay on the floor and copied it out by ear and then used to sleep with it under his pillow.

Aged five he gave his first recital at the Municipal Theatre. As always in these countries, it began late and he was very tired, but when his sister lifted him on to the stool, that tiredness left him completely. This little prodigy was fêted everywhere.

He was hailed as a second Mozart, and the Chilean government paid for the whole family to go to Berlin so he could study there, but at first he experienced indifferent teaching and began to lose interest. The Chilean pianist, Rosita Renard, who was performing there at the time, heard him and took him to play for Martin Krause (1853 – 1919) who had been studying with Liszt in Weimar for the last five years of that great musician's life, and in fact, had processed at Liszt's funeral. Martin Krause wrote of Arrau, "The greatest pianistic talent since Franz Liszt. He plays as Liszt did," and he devoted himself to the young boy, looking after every single aspect of his education and growth, musical and otherwise. He later got him into the Stern Conservatory to teach at the age of sixteen by writing of him, "He is engrossed with his whole soul and his enthusiasm for his art and that is the most important factor for one of his age. Not only outwardly, but inwardly, this boy is thoroughly endowed for the highest artistic endeavour, which always is, and always was, the origin of great deeds."

Krause was adamant he had to practise technique every single day, and that anyone who did not was just a 'talented amateur'. But realising that the boy played just like Liszt he wisely decided to leave Arrau's technique alone. He just made sure he worked assiduously at all technical aspects. No other student played in the same way as Arrau. He moved around the piano like a cat. He had the admiration of another student of Krause's, Edwin Fischer, who had become Krause's assistant at the Stern, and who was six or seven years older than Claudio.

The Arraus lived in a house in the same street as the Krauses, but really he only slept there, spending all his days in his master's home with the five daughters, where he practised, ate, read, and had lessons for two or three hours after Krause arrived back from the Stern. Krause attended to every single detail regarding Arrau...diet, physical exercise, very long walks in all weathers, visits to libraries, theatres, great art galleries, much literature and language...and of course, his music. He was the father figure in Arrau's life.

Claudio knew the entire Forty-Eight Preludes and Fugues by the age of twelve. At the same age he was given the 'Eroica Variations', 'Mazeppa' and 'Feux Follets' to be learned in one week. They were the hardest of works and he simply couldn't master them in the time, at which Krause was displeased. The boy sobbed and had to be consoled by the daughters. As a consequence he was uncomfortable with Mazeppa for years. Krause pushed on him a huge repertoire.

He spoke five languages, saw and took in Parsifal at eight years of age, but apart from walking, never enjoyed any sports and never ever understood what children's play was all about. On his walks he used to see children playing in a park and simply could not understand what they were doing!

I was once coming out of a building in London with him, and there was a huge press sign, "England annihilated by the Aussies", and Arrau was greatly alarmed. "Ruthie, what is this? Something terrible has happened!" I had to explain to him it was about a Test Cricket Match. He was astounded. A game? No, he could not understand any such thing. (Ironically, later one of his closest friends was Neville Cardus, who was not only a great music critic but also a great cricket writer.) On another occasion I sat with him over lunch at the Savoy and tried hard to explain to him the subtleties of a spin bowler and a fast bowler. He listened very intently, then said, "But Ruthie, it's only a game!" He simply could not grasp the fact that the special skills I had been talking about needed intense practice, just as the perfection of movements for musicians, gymnasts and tennis players did. It didn't just happen; it needed great and intense practice over a long time. I gave up!

Arrau was very serious about his performances. He always gave them his full self, his full dedication. Once in London we were leaving the Savoy Hotel at about 6pm when we ran into Arthur Rubenstein who was just returning after a shopping expedition, laden with parcels. Of course the two maestros fell into each other's arms with great warmth and excitement. Then Rubenstein excused himself. "I must go and get changed. I have a performance at the Royal Festival Hall at 7.30pm." It was then 6pm! As we walked away, Arrau was absolutely staggered. This delightful, casual attitude was just not part of Arrau's makeup. He always had a ritual preparation for concerts. Two great artists...two different attitudes!

In Berlin, lots of concerts for Arrau had been organised by Krause...fifteen to twenty per season. He gave his first Berlin recital in 1914 and in 1915 played the Liszt E flat with the Dresden Orchestra under Nikisch. Strangely there was very little mention of WW1, probably because he was too young and too sheltered at the time. In 1919 Krause died – a victim of the disastrous influenza epidemic that swept through Europe. Arrau was sixteen and absolutely shattered. He was adamant he would never have another teacher. This of course stopped the financial support from the Chilean Government because he was no longer a student, and it was the beginning of a time of enormous hardship because Arrau was now the man of the household and needed to provide for his family. Not enough food, never money for public transport, enormous feelings of responsibility, self-doubt and depression, and every day he said he wondered if he could carry on. In later life, Claudio Arrau said that in retrospect he was very glad he had suffered the hopelessness of those times as it had taught him so much about life. Where was the much older brother Carlos, who had travelled with the family to Berlin? I have seen an early family photograph of the three and references to him in various books, but no one seems to know what happened to him. Claudio only ever talked of his sister.

In 1919 and 1920 he twice won the Liszt prize, and that helped a bit financially. Without Krause's influence, however, concerts began to dry up and the prodigy aspect was dying too as he became a young man, losing that child appeal.

Somehow he was helped to perform on tours in Chile and Argentina, but again not much success financially. Once on tour in South America all his travel connections were late and he missed the scheduled rehearsal, but though arriving late and breathless, the conductor said, "Well, now you are here, we might as well perform the concerto." Hurriedly sitting down at the piano, Arrau opened his hands in the position to play the first G Major chord of the Beethoven 4th, and the orchestra started the opening notes of the C minor one! His comment was, "Thank God it was a long orchestral tutti and I could get my thoughts in order!" But just think about the preparedness of this man...that he was able in an instant to move from one concerto to another that he could play on the spot just as well!

In 1922, managed by Harold Holt, he made his first visit to London, sharing the stage at the Royal Albert Hall with Dame Nellie Melba. The audience brought him back again and again, but suddenly he felt a large hand on his shoulder. "That's enough, Boy," hissed Melba as she marched out on to the stage herself!

In 1923 there was the disastrous trip to the USA, very badly organised from Berlin. He had to pay all his own expenses, got into considerable debt and it was only through the kindness of the Baldwin Piano Company (New York), who paid his fare that he was able to get home. It didn't stop there. The Berlin agent insisted he pay off all he had spent on the tour even though he, the agent, had organised it so ineffectively. When Claudio told him he had no money whatsoever, he demanded that he write off this debt by giving his daughter weekly lessons for however long it took. Screwing up his face as only Arrau could, he related... "She was terrible. <u>And</u> she was so ugly!" He was so grateful to Baldwin that he paid tribute to this company by having one of their pianos in his studio in New York; I used to practise on this.

In 1927 he was called upon to replace the great Schnabel under Klemperer with the Schumann Concerto. At the pianist's entry of the first subject, on the first page, Klemperer stopped him and said, "You can't play it like that, Boy. Go to the artists' room and I will come and speak to you there." He was so young. Alone in this room he agonised over the situation. "The great Klemperer...do I do what he says? Or do I stay true to what I believe is correct?" He truly agonised over this, but finally decided he must remain true to himself. Nervously but politely and firmly he finally told the conductor, "Herr Doctor, if I cannot play it like this I cannot play it at all." Interestingly, Klemperer accepted this outcome and brought him back on stage. (Perhaps the courage and musical integrity of the young man impressed him?)

In 1927 he won the well rewarded Geneva Competition, so he was slowly beginning to survive financially.

1933 saw a trip to Mexico with fifteen recitals and four concertos. From Mexico he went to Venezuela, where they had no experience of concert pianists at all. Dreadful living conditions, dirty halls, and on to Trinidad, where rather surprisingly there were great recitals with huge audiences. He played in Poland, Finland, the Baltic states, but not so often now in Germany. He worried about this and knew he had to do something to try to re-establish himself in Berlin. So he decided to offer the Complete Keyboard Works of J.S. Bach. He performed this between October 1935 and June 1936 and during this enormous marathon, he told me rather proudly, he made only one tiny slip, which was in one of the Partitas.

During this time he met Ruth and wanted to court her but he told her he must complete the Bach project first. He loved dancing but did not invite her dancing in case she could not. She also loved dancing but rather worried he did not! Finally they worked that one out and enjoyed going dining and dancing together. They were married in 1937 and she remained the rock in his life right throughout their long time together. There were three children in the family.

In Germany Arrau also performed the complete works of Beethoven, Weber and Schubert.

Life in Berlin was becoming more and more worrisome under the increasing power of the Nazis. Ruth had little Carmen aged two, and because there were found to be complications with her second pregnancy, they were forced to remain behind when Arrau left Germany to tour the USA with plans for her to follow immediately the baby was born. She was in the care of life-long friend and colleague, Rafael de Silva, and the four of them (with babe in arms) managed to get out of Germany on the very last train to Spain and then she had to take the children down to Arrau's mother in Chile and stay with this dominating woman for quite some time. It was extremely difficult for her. Claudio was already in New York, trying to get an American career (and income) started and had to find a family home for them. Later they were all reunited there and Rafael later became Arrau's much trusted and admired professional assistant. He had been a very good pianist whose crippling pre-concert nerves had prevented a well deserved public career. de Silva was exceptional. He fully understood the subtle qualities of the piano and the way to put across the very basics of the technique required to realise this...perhaps even better than Arrau. I had a very good experience with Rafael de Silva because I worked very hard and I understood him; but I heard stories from others who had found him very difficult and volatile.

In 1941 Arrau was triumphant at Carnegie Hall. He also secured a recording contract with RCA with whom he did the Bach Goldberg Variations, Chromatic Fantasy and Fugue, Symphonias and Inventions. Then Landowska arrived in New York and RCA asked him if he would postpone the release of his recording of the Goldberg Variations. Arrau agreed because he had huge admiration for Landowska and also had a nagging doubt himself about playing Bach on the piano. In the meantime he had signed with CBC. When he finally listened to the RCA master tapes he found that he was absolutely happy with them. He decided that Bach could indeed be well played on the piano, so long as one knew how.

There was only one composer he didn't care too much about, and that was Rachmaninov. This was, he said, because "No matter what he plays, it always becomes Rachmaninov." But Arrau had a secret. Once in South America, when he had been terribly hard up, he took part in a film, playing the Rachmaninov Second Concerto as background music. "Don't tell anyone," he had joked. He had to find a home for the family in New York. One agent showed him a house and proudly told him it had been rented by Rachmaninov – so that was the end of that! He finally found their home on Long Island Sound, and this is what he bought, and is where the family lived from that time on.

His career at this time was taken over by Friede Rothe. She was a superb woman and PA, loyal and devoted to her few artists. When she telephoned us in London her booming voice could be heard right across the Atlantic! Under Friede Rothe's management, Arrau was now giving one hundred and fifty concerts a year all over the world.

To return to musical life in Berlin, Busoni had settled there in 1894 and was teacher of Composition at the Academy of Arts...Arrau greatly admired Busoni's breadth and imagination. His pupil, Kurt Weill, taught Arrau Composition. It was actually Kurt Weill who once remarked, "Pretty Boy Claudio Arrau arrived today with a moustache!" Arrau kept a moustache from the time he grew his first for the rest of his life. Furtwangler, conductor of the Berlin Philharmonic, died in 1954. Schoenberg, who had taken over from Busoni, died in 1951 and Schnabel came from Vienna in 1922. Edwin Fischer had also come from Vienna and had settled in Berlin earlier...in 1904.

After the Nazi experiences, Arrau loved his perception of the vision of freedom in New York, the vibrancy, theatres, museums and their "Freedom of Man" mentality. He hated the provincial American states though. Arrau said, "Columbia Artists only ever wanted popular works, and there it was full of blue-rinsed ladies and you could never get decent food!" He loved Australia. He and Ruth Arrau travelled there for ABC tours; the ABC and Israel tours were the toughest he ever did. He was fond of saying, "I speak five languages. But in Australia I was always saying 'Pardon?'...when I first arrived I found it difficult to tune into the Australian accent!"

...to move onto my time studying with Arrau...

As he could be away for up to six weeks at a time, the spacing of lessons was excellent for someone like me. I told Rafael de Silva what I wished to perform for the maestro and it gave me time to prepare totally so there was never an area or one tiny indication in the score which for someone at my standard as a performing artist to have overlooked would have been immensely embarrassing to say the least! Arrau never charged for his lessons.

There would usually be five of us, and despite just having arrived back from touring and being tired, he would arrive, always absolutely dapper in appearance, sitting a little away from the piano and teaching us with his voice, his facial expressions, his hands and his arm movements. He never used a second instrument. He taught 95% musically and interpretively. Hand gestures, and his amazing sense of imagery and memory and the background depth of his experience and insight were just wonderful. He was unfailingly kind but firm, only once ever losing his temper with someone. (This was when he had taken the trouble to give his own particular fingering to the young man who was continuing to have difficulty with a passage and at the next lesson the same pianist had not used it, saying he found it 'awkward'...Arrau was outraged!) His aim was for us not only to know the technical and physical way to create sound, but to enjoy and to explore the image of this sound in our heads, leaving our technical ability to transfer that into and through the instrument.

He used to tell us, "At your level as performing artists, you should have such a technique mastered, the gymnastics of the piano as it were, and you should never be surprised by your sound, good or bad. You should know this before your hands reach the keys, the quality and the quantity. You should trust your technique to achieve this, but of course technique must always be your servant, never your master. You should not need to think about technique at this level when performing or it will interfere with the process of creation."

Getting down to his principles, it was really very simple...only several important movements to know about.

1. *Arm Weight. Up or down...elbows in a natural position with the wrist and hand remaining absolutely flexible.*
2. *Lateral Movement.*
3. *Circles...using the wrist.*
4. *Creation of Legato. Not just playing the notes connected. It is preparing each note and weight-shifting for the next*

note through the arm and hand. You must never rely upon the pedal as a crutch. The pedal is there to produce extra colour. It must be bel canto, as Chopin used in his teaching. Remember a run is a melody too. Phrase through your arm and body. Legato double notes: In your weight shifting, have a very soft hand and both parts must move equally legato.

5. *Finger strength...*
   (Arrau had an absolute horror of typewriter style finger technique! He couldn't stand it!)

Claudio Arrau had fingers of steel but they could be as light as goose down, warm, tender, noble, ironic, spiteful, grand, and all this proving that the fingers are the last element and completely the servant of one's imagination and the using of one's body. Arrau showed a great variety of emotion on his face when he played, but there were never any empty gestures for showing off as many pianists do. I believe body language must be absolutely genuine. I always stress the importance of intelligent fingering. Pupils who don't know the exact fingering they are using and so can't tell you immediately, find it very difficult to change when a more logical or imaginative fingering is suggested.

Cheating: He detested it in any work whatsoever. By this he meant in passages, which were extremely difficult to manage with one hand, to split between two hands. He was not being a spoilsport. He pointed out that the difficulty placed there by the composer always had a purpose. The tension created by this same difficulty added to the artistic and musical tension of the passage, which the composer had usually completely understood and intended. If you try to make it easier for yourself that intended tension will not be there. It will sound facile at the best. Not only that, but it always creates another difficulty...not intended.

Interpretation: A real interpreter is someone who can transform himself into something he is not. He/she must be able to overcome all barriers, historical, emotional, geographical and stylistic. Don't be typecast. Interpretation begins after honest dedicated assimilation of the composer's markings and intentions, personal historical background, other arts and literature of the time. Then, and only then, you may add a little of yourself. You must have the capacity to submerge yourself in different worlds.

Arrau was an obsessive seeker of truth his entire life. He was a strange mixture of inner command, control, self-assurance, aware of his own unique qualities, but never arrogant. But he could also be completely child-like, very stubborn (and how!) and even have the occasional tantrum, and often showed a lack of ease with strangers. When travelling with him I had to deal with all this and manage it somehow. As he got older, the tiniest mishap in performance became an inconsolable worry. And he often threatened to cancel a performance. I 'saved' some of them by just managing him with, shall we say, finely tuned diplomacy.

After a concert, he needed to 'come down'. He changed into his après-concert cloak and then liked to meet people, so dinners in such circumstances became very late affairs. Once I recall he was utterly bemused because a woman had come to his dressing room and had said, "Oh maestro, that was so nice." In reporting this to me, he burst out laughing and said, "Nice? Nice? It can be a lot of things, but surely never 'nice'!"

Practising: When I was performing I used to practise six or seven hours daily. Arrau used to say, "The only part of your body which should become tired after many hours of practice is your brain, never your hands or your body. If it does, you are doing it wrongly. And you should be able to play every work ten times faster and ten times slower than is required for a performance." (slight exaggeration)

Arrau could never understand artists who needed to warm up before a performance. He never did. He used to say that if called upon to do so one should be ready to perform even at 2am!

Stamina: He would ask, "How many times can you play the Chopin Study No1 repeatedly? And play all those etudes in different keys?"

And he remarked that performers who fight the piano have entirely the wrong approach.

It worries me that today's generation of piano students do not totally understand the need for daily technical practice, the vital importance of total gymnastic command of the keyboard. You should be like a ballet dancer exercising daily at the barre...at the piano and considering your posture too.

Arrau said, "When the technical aspect is mastered, one can reach out for the essence of the music, and not before. Technical difficulties block interpretation. If we are to perform, we should never wonder how to do it. We must know this 100% first."

To me, Arrau's hands always looked as though there were no bones in them. He had an amazing thumb that could bend back away from the second finger towards the wrist. So in fast octave passages he would use 2,3,4,5. Makes life easy!!

Once when we were out he slammed a car door on his hand...but it became nothing...just 'disappeared' it seemed. And he made nothing of it at all.

He told me so many wise things when we were travelling together. I was learning from him all the time. There are things he said which I treasure, like...

"My dear, everything is heightened with age. There is no lessening of feelings, of passion or intellect...just maybe a little less physicality."

and

"You know Ruthie, as we get older, our muscles become wiser. They may lose a little physically, but they are wiser."

My ideas about performing and about teaching were enormously enhanced by my years with Arrau.

....

Ruth Arrau died of complications from diabetes. The last time Ross and I saw them both was at their Douglaston home and they were both looking very elegant. She was a smart dresser as was Arrau, but it was clear to us she was a very ill woman.

After the death of the rock and love of his life, Arrau was devastated and didn't play in public again, and not bearing to remain at Douglaston, moved to a small village near Munich. He said, "From now on I will only do some recordings. My heart for performance has gone."

On June 9th, 1991, he was lunching with his friend and assistant, and afterwards suffered great stomach pain, which he blamed on the fish. He said it would pass, so nothing was done till the next morning when the pain was still acute and he seemed really ill. He underwent surgery, but unfortunately died several hours later.

The world lost one of the greatest musicians of the twentieth century. Those of you in this audience who are my students are beneficiaries of the following unbroken and priceless heritage:

I studied with Claudio Arrau.

Arrau studied with Martin Krause.

Martin Krause studied with Liszt.

Liszt studied with Czerny.

Czerny studied with Beethoven.

Beethoven studied with Haydn.

We have this unbroken line going right back to 18th century Haydn. It is a precious and valuable heritage of which we are privileged to be part. If you value it you also will feel a responsibility to pass it on to those who come after you.

MY TIME WITH
ARRAU LECTURE TWO

February 6th, 2006

The second lecture was filmed and the following is a combination of Ruth's words and my observations.

In this second lecture, a year later, Ruth Nye is getting down to the actual matter of technique and has some of her students standing by. These students have no idea what will be asked of them.

....

Claudio Arrau, had he lived, would have been 103 today.

Last time we were here together, (incredibly an entire year ago) I told you about his life and my very long association with this remarkable man and great musician. This time I would like to concentrate on his importance as a very great teacher, and how privileged I was to inherit his ideas and to have been able to pass on this valuable heritage to my concert students and others. My own very long experience as a teacher has overlapped this heritage, so my teaching now is truly a combination of the two.

Arrau disliked the idea of any 'Arrau School' of teaching and performing. He never considered himself better than other international concert pianists. He just knew that his way of playing the piano was different, and it was this difference he was prepared to pass on to a very select few.

When he was teaching in Berlin at the Stern Conservatory (from as early as sixteen years till he left Germany in 1940), he already knew that his sound was different, and he really wanted to find out what, physically, helped him create that particular and personal sound, so he might be able to teach it to his students. All he knew was that his body behaved differently from other performers. He went to the extreme of setting up mirrors around himself when he practised and spent hours studying his demeanour at the piano so that he could pass on this valuable information to students. There is no doubt that his handling of his own body, his weight transference, the way he 'crawled' along the keyboard, helped him create the wonderful and distinctive sound he made.

Arrau had an abhorrence for the idea of imitating. He stressed that all performers were different, had different bodies, different hands, and he taught how to adapt what a performer had, and assisted them to attain the highest level whilst retaining their own personality in performance. His whole view of teaching was to encourage you to do it your way, but with the increased insight and knowledge he was able to give, and the knowledge of how to produce the desired sound.

What I teach is improvement of the equipment (physical) and knowledge and insight, which enable a better performance. But I don't ever wish to alter a musical personality. And destructive criticism is always to be avoided. I regard destructive teaching as being the easiest kind of teaching, and it can have disastrous results. You must always give the person the flexibility to grow.

Arrau had the ability to understand all personal problems too...the psychological ones particularly. He had been through much of that himself. He had the wonderful balance between self-belief and lack of arrogance. Above all, his interest was in the composer of any work, and the composer's intentions. His humility was notable.

Arrau was Chilean. I am glad also that I was born an Australian. And therefore we can dispense with this nonsense that only Viennese can play Schubert properly, only the Polish can play Chopin, and only Germans can play Beethoven for example.

Arrau used to say, "In interpretation, you have to be able to transform yourself into something you are not. You have to be able to step into any nationality and into any period...and you have to do it with intelligence and dedication."

Arrau regarded absolute adherence to the score to be of the utmost importance, and so do I. How often have you known me to ask questions relating to what is actually there in the score, and which is being ignored? And how often have I asked about terms, and titles, and when not known, demanded they be researched? Sometimes the answers I am given are really amusing...for example, particularly when some-one says to me, 'I looked it up on the Internet and there was nothing.' (Again that wonderful ringing laugh!) *"Anyone who knows my lack of skills on the Internet would know what anathema that is to me! Have you tried a book perhaps? They are still around, you know!"*

Interpretation:

Arrau used to say, "Whatever the music needs in emotion, drama, even in virtuosity, give it...but never impose it." This is a most important quotation and should be remembered. Shall I repeat it?

He was against copying recordings. He used to say, "Maybe listen to it once, then put it away. Learn the work yourself thoroughly from the score. Only when you know the work 100% thoroughly from the score, can you dare attempt some interpretation of your own." Of course we can learn from great performers, but wait until you have ideas of your own.

His advice regarding interpretation was utterly invaluable. It also greatly involved the use of one's imagination. Without using one's imagination, a work can sound lifeless, even boring, whilst at the same time being correct. I have so often had students come for an audition, and play for me something demanding, which is absolutely correct...but which bores me. I remember suggesting to a gifted young boy of about twelve that he replay the first eight bars or so of his Bartok whilst thinking of being on a barren wind-swept landscape and feeling terribly alone and sad. He looked at me for a few moments and then repeated these bars, and it was wonderful. It was just so different.

Technique:

(Here, it looks as though Ruth has reached perhaps the most important focus of this lecture. She goes on to discuss aspects of technique but has requested that I confine some of this to the discussions in " Conversations with Ruth Nye", which follows later.)

Arrau always said that fear is the greatest enemy and preventer of beautiful interpretation. Fear comes about when one knows one has any technical problems, even slight ones. To avoid the presence of destructive fear, technique must be perfected and it can only be perfected with daily, rigorous practice.

I often ask my students to consider the fact that all our bodies and hands and shapes are so different. But we must learn to adapt these physical differences to enable us to perform well. And to enable us to adapt them, we need to know about them, and how to adapt them. This needs a lot of thought…the brain is very important when learning anything…never more so than in learning technique.

(Here she asks various students to come forward and to compare body size, hand size and length of arm.)

Remember, your brain is the most important part of your body when it comes to playing. Your brain needs to send the right messages to the different parts of the body in order for there to be a satisfying performance.

Editions:

Arrau loved Schnabel and his editions. But he always used to say, "Learn the work thoroughly from the urtext first. And maybe *after that, you can go to the various good editions and see if there are worthwhile suggestions, which you might make use of. But always remember, these are <u>editions</u>."*

Back to Technique:

We don't just play the piano with our hands; we play with our bodies....our bodies, informed firstly by our brains. Arrau used to say, "You should never be surprised by the sound you have just produced. You should always know with security how the sound will be if you have used your body, including your arms and hands, the correct way to produce it."

Like Chopin, he believed in the bel canto *quality of the piano. Sure...it is a large percussive instrument. But it is so much more than that, isn't it? We can make it sound like any instrument of the orchestra...if we know how. We are so fortunate in this. We are privileged.*

Weight and Freedom:

(Here Ruth talks about (and demonstrates) all the muscles in the back, wrists, hands, and how all must be <u>free</u>.)

If they are not free, i.e. if you don't have the back and all other parts free first, you will have a locked wrist, and with a locked wrist, no good quality of sound will emerge. You might play the notes correctly enough, but the quality of the sound will not be what you want. You want the note to ring, and if the back is not right, it won't happen, because none of the other things from the shoulders and back onwards will have happened.

(Ruth is demonstrating on her own body how to interpret these remarks.)

I often say it takes three notes to make one: the one you come from, the one you play and the one you move to.

(She then goes to the piano to demonstrate her next point... movement from one note to another.)

Every note needs to be <u>prepared</u> by a movement from the preceding one.

(Ruth demonstrates the movement necessary for this to be so. It is called weight-transference. She then calls Miho, who is very slight in build, to the piano to demonstrate weight-handling in playing chords...dropping the weight down and pushing up with each chord.)

The sound Miho gets from these chords has nothing to do with her size. It's all about how she has learned to use the weight she needs to produce the full musical sound of those chords rather than just playing the chords any old way, and having any old quality of sound emerge. The weight goes up and the weight comes down, and if you learn how to do this effectively, you are never wasting any energy. It's simple really. You just need to learn how to do it, and then you will know how to use the piano to produce the best results.

There was a time when some misguided people imagined Arrau was teaching about playing the piano with no tension at all. Well of course that was all nonsense. There has to be some tension....you cannot do anything physical without some tension. But you have to learn how to control and release that same tension, or the quality of the sound will not be good.

Legato:

(She talks about how Arrau played legato and how she teaches it.)

What is the magic of this? It is all about weight-shifting. How do we weight-shift? We make circles with our hands and arms, keeping it alive through the entire arm. "Trust your arms," I tell my students. "If you don't trust them, it won't happen."

(She demonstrates a fairly well connected scale...which seems ok...it's not wrong, but it is not absolutely and entirely legato either. A discerning ear hears the difference. She then talks, and demonstrates scales in double thirds, which are supposed to be legato.)

Here you have two parts moving up the keyboard together. You want the progression to be absolutely legato. To achieve absolute legato thirds, <u>both</u> parts have to move in an absolutely legato way all the time...not just the upper part. The fingering used is so important for this.

Fingering:

The vexed matter of fingering is probably the one thing which causes Ruth sometimes to feel despair. The most appropriate fingering to use for any passage is a most important consideration, and she is always amazed when a student obviously has not thought this through totally and individually. She does not wish always to tell them; she would much prefer them to think it out themselves and to make definite changes if the printed fingering does not suit their hands. When she sees the pupils achieve this she is delighted. Most fingering in scores are written by editors for their own hands.

Chopin had very firm ideas about fingering, and suggested that we must acknowledge the personality of all the different fingers, taking into consideration the different strengths of every finger, particularly the 4th and 5th ones, and to use that difference accordingly, and then the different quality of sound produced by each can be very beneficial. Whenever we are using the 4th and 5th fingers we must acknowledge that yes, they are the weaker ones, and we must crescendo just that small amount towards them every time. In my experience, students who don't know their fingering, never have the ability to change or to use different fingering or to discover the joys of thinking about one's fingering.

The Wrist (Maybe the body part which produces the most problems):

I always tell my students that the wrist is like their lungs. If it is stiff, the muscles there are not getting the oxygen they need and so don't breathe, and the wrist therefore becomes locked. And a locked wrist is the greatest enemy to the production of a beautiful quality of sound. Everything must be fluid. The muscles and joints in the fingers must absolutely disappear... after one has learned all about them and knows how to make them as strong as steel. Steely fingers are essential. And then the knowledge how to have steely fingers without seeming to! Too hard to understand? Well, you just need to know. You just need to come to my weekly technique classes for a start! 8 o'clock on Thursday mornings... Often I think I am the only one fully awake at that hour! (Again the joyous ringing laugh and everyone joins in.)

Lateral Movement:

We have talked about Circular Movements, but when do we also need that other most important facet of piano technique, Lateral Movements? Yes...in trilling especially.

She asks Emmanuel to demonstrate the lateral movements necessary for the trilling drill he has devised for himself. It is utterly amazing....between every combination of fingers in every key. All performed with perfect ease, equality, and strength.

This is his own work...his own ideas...his own creation. You can do the same. It may not be as complicated and sophisticated as Emmanuel's, but work out your own exercises, to suit your own level, for your own technical drill, and do it every single day of your life. If you don't, you will never be more than a 'talented amateur' as Krause says. And those of you in this room who are studying with me at either the Yehudi Menuhin School or the RCM are not interested in just being talented amateurs, are you? You are hoping for, or are already on the way to, musical careers.

Emmanuel has shown you trilling for strength of fingers, but now I would like him to demonstrate the kind of lateral movements necessary for other types of trilling.

(He plays parts of a big work (the Brahms Concerto on which he is working), which has very big trills of another type, and she is satisfied.)

Now Miho, would you come forward again and would you demonstrate for us what I would call a <u>seductive trill</u> please?

(Ruth then reminds her audience that none of what these students has demonstrated has been in any way rehearsed...that they came here today having no idea what they might be asked to do. Miho thinks for a moment and then plays the opening of the gorgeous Debussy 'L'Isle Joyeuse' with its delicate, sensuous trills....yes indeed they could be so called 'seductive' trills! Ruth goes on to talk about not wasting energy at the piano.)

Don't leave the keys. Stay close to them, almost in the key-bed. If you move away too much, you always need to return, and that is wasting energy. When do you need to think about how to use your elbow? You use your elbow when you want to make a leap.

(She demonstrates leaps...with and without the correct use of the elbow.)

Using the elbow the correct way aids a much quicker leap. Watch a cat: it eyes what it is going to jump to and then suddenly leaps….never makes a mistake. Or watch birds: they suddenly swoop down and land on a very thin wire...never making a mistake...never saying, "Oh dear, not quite feeling up to it today, a bit wobbly today, or oops, I'm going to fall off!" No, never. You must never make a mistake when you leap on the keyboard either, and if you use your elbow correctly, you won't. But, as I said, it all starts up here...in the head.

When I first went to Arrau he asked me what Liszt I had played and I answered, "Oh, I haven't done much Liszt because I have rather small hands." He was staggered. "What nonsense!" he said..."Size of hands has nothing whatsoever to do with it. And I would much prefer to work through very big works with a musician with small hands than with someone who has large hands. The large-handed ones tend to get lazy...and also their large hands create further particular technical problems for them."

Any pianist with very large hands and long fingers has a different kind of technical problem in that he often needs to curve those fingers or he would be hitting the wood! It does create its own set of problems to be solved..

The Pedal:

Oh dear...the pedal!

The great Busoni described the pedal as being The Soul of The Piano. Think about that. The Soul of the Piano. Please don't use it, as so many people do, simply as a crutch. The pedal is the greatest help for colouring...it is the most imaginative of your entire palette of colours. But you must know how to use it correctly in order to produce the colours, which are needed. And remember also, you don't pedal with your foot...you pedal with your ear. Listen always for the sound you want.

Posture:

When you have embarked upon the long journey towards becoming a concert pianist obviously you are going to need to practise for very long hours. Your body must be kept fit in order to be able to accomplish these long hours at the piano without undue stress and without any physical damage to your muscles and various parts of the body. This is obvious, isn't it? You need the right kinds of physical exercise. Stamina is an all-important consideration.

I believe that posture at the piano is one of the most important considerations for a performer. Tension must not be there. Easy enough to say, but remarkably difficult to achieve. The back is just so important. We hold ourselves up by the small of the back and therefore it is the small of the back, which so often takes most of the strain during long hours of practice. To lessen the possibility of an aching back, which then translates into pain elsewhere in the parts of the body involved in playing the piano, we should get up every hour or so and move around, limbering up, and relieving any tension we notice.

The shoulders must be down...never coming up when there is a difficult passage to manipulate!

(How often I have seen Ruth Nye in a lesson walk over and very gently push a student's shoulders down...just as a kind of reminder. How well indeed I remember her doing the same to me during sessions I have spent with her. My shoulders, without my being in any way conscious of it, apparently would rise slightly during a particularly tricky passage.)

So once again, it is the brain which must be involved first of all...the brain is constantly reminding a serious piano student how to sit, how to manage back, shoulders, legs, arms and wrists and hands, so tension can be avoided. This can be learned. Arrau used to say that one's body should never be made tired by long hours of practice...one's mind perhaps, but never one's body, so long as the technique for using it correctly has been well achieved. He used to say, "My hands are never tired."

(For those of us less virtuosic, this might appear a non-achievable aim, but after years of study with Ruth Nye her advanced concert students, and those already performing publicly, will verify that it is most certainly achievable…once you know how.)

Ideally you should become part of the instrument…being part of the organic whole…the entire sweep of performer and instrument. Not just sitting there at the piano and playing. And this too involves posture, and the right shoes (never, please, very high heels, which upset the balance of the body at the piano), and the ability of being able to convey mentally to the listener that you are indeed part of the instrument itself. It is so much more of a challenge with a great big instrument like the piano: whereas the violinists, the cellists etc., can hug, caress, and be more obviously part of their own instruments, the pianists need to think this concept through more and to make themselves part of that whole.

Ruth then talks more about methods of practising technique and how she worries that the topic is not given the attention due to it in so many music-teaching institutions.

Her students, from a very early age, right through to concert standard, are encouraged to work out for themselves various patterns which form a basis for practice of particular technical problems and also which are related to the particular works they are learning to master. She herself also gives them ideas, but she much prefers to encourage the brain work required for her gifted students to be able to devise these things themselves.

She brings forward six-year-old little Ursula (*It is marvellous when you can get them so young!*), who was so delighted when she worked out for herself a means of matching shapes of phrases to the fingerings she gave them. She showed the audience she had also worked out that she could play the scale of C Major, hands together, but with the RH playing in fours, while the LH played in threes, and then vice versa. This excited her so much she couldn't wait to demonstrate this to her teacher at her last lesson, and of course delighted her teacher too.

I was even happier about her own excitement at having tried and achieved this than I was about the actual achievement.

The audience showed they were excited by her performance too. Ruth has a special place in her heart for the very young gifted students. She rarely accepts them, but when she is aware of something very special, it is a labour of love to be able to participate in and nurture their development.

Next to be introduced is nineteen-year-old Melissa, who was practising a Ligeti work for the Finals of the BBC Young Musician of the Year Competition later in the month. The work consists of constant complicated canons. So Melissa illustrated the technical drills she had put together for herself which would assist her performance...two hands in double thirds, but in canon...one following the other. All in different keys. Incredible! Professor Nye looks suitably pleased. *"See? She is using her brain."*

She then tells of how she had overheard Miho, whilst she was staying with them at Longfrey, practising scales which to Ruth's ear (elsewhere in the house) sounded a bit "different". When asked about it, Miho said, "Well I was practising scales on all the black notes, but using C Major fingering." And of course it included the majors, minors, melodic minors, arpeggios both major and minor, and dominant and diminished sevenths... commencing on every one of the black notes, but always using the white C Major fingering. Amazing?

You see? She has listened to my advice and is using her brain. Your fingers will only go as fast as your brain; otherwise they are out of control.

To finish this lecture, Ruth Nye asks if there are any questions, and several are put forward, which she answers succinctly. When asked if Arrau had been interested in Harmonic Analysis, she laughed and answered,

Goodness yes! One could never compartmentalise...with him aspects could never be divorced. He would say for example, "Go back to the Diminished Seventh chord which introduces the section where it goes into F minor." You simply had to know these things. You would have been acutely embarrassed otherwise.

Asked if there was any composer of whom Arrau was not fond, she thought for a moment before answering,

Yes. Rachmaninov. Why? He thought he was too over the top (though generally he loved Russian music) and perhaps...um...his music was often....

She paused, and someone called out "musical mush" and she laughed and said maybe that had been it.

....

Terry Lewis brings this lecture to a close by thanking Ruth and telling the audience he loved her very much, as we all do, and she had for many years been the greatest inspiration, teacher and mentor to him. Finally he said,

As well, I have sat in on so many of your lessons over the years, and travelled all over Europe to appointments when necessary with you (carrying your bags!) and so I can fully appreciate how you would have continued to absorb and learn

from the maestro when you were travelling with him for so many years. In conversations, in observance, one is learning all the time. So our thanks to you, dear Ruth, for all you have given us, and continue to give us, and may we be fortunate enough to continue to receive your wisdom and assistance for many years to come.

....

THE ROYAL COLLEGE OF MUSIC

Andrew Ball, former Head of Keyboard, asked Ruth to join the piano faculty at the Royal College of Music in 2001, where she now teaches two days a week.

The College, a delightful red brick building (the same brickwork as the Royal Albert Hall opposite), is situated on Kensington Gore, in London's cultural heartland of South Kensington. It is close to not only the Albert Hall, but also to the Royal College of Art, Imperial College of London, and the Victoria and Albert Museum. It is one of the world's leading conservatories. Founded in 1882 by the Prince of Wales (later Edward VII), the RCM has trained gifted musicians from all over the world for international careers as performers, conductors, and composers and other significant leadership roles within the arts. Many of its graduates are at the very forefront of the international music scene. The RCM's professors are all musicians with worldwide reputations, accustomed to working with the most talented students of each generation to unlock their artistic potential. The College's influence on the development of music over the past 125 plus years is incalculable, and looks to the future with great enthusiasm.

Her Majesty Queen Elizabeth is currently its patron and since 1993, HRH The Prince of Wales its president. It was The Prince of Wales who presented Emmanuel Despax with the College's coveted Tagore Medal.

Many of Ruth's students have won awards and prizes and topped their years. These include the Chappell Medal at both the Royal Academy of Music (where Ruth was formerly on the staff) and the Royal College of Music.

Ruth Nye's teaching-room on the second floor is large and sunny, with two grand pianos, one Steinway and one Fazioli, and looks out directly at the beautiful building of the Royal Albert Hall across the large court in between. What a view!

....

"Ruth is a very special person. She is one of the most brilliant piano teachers and has a natural caring quality that sets her apart from the rest."

Professor Vanessa Latarche, FRCM, Head of Keyboard since 2005

KALEIDOSCOPE

It's actually necessary to be an experienced musician oneself in order to perceive and understand the changes and developments, which take place in Ruth's students as a direct consequence of her teaching. For many years I have been privileged to have observed many lessons at the London Mews, the Yehudi Menuhin School, the Royal College of Music and at Longfrey Farm. It has always been inspiring for me, as well as being a learning experience in itself, to witness at first hand Ruth's gifts of communication, imagery, literary references and technical guidance as well as profound musical insight. Her choice of words is memorable; I find myself reflecting on them long afterwards, finding they have stimulated my own thoughts about the works. She finds the right words to trigger their imaginations – for everyone it is different. This imagery is so alive and so realistic. They know what she means…they are intelligent and respond immediately both to her words and to her actions. Ruth's students are led by her to find their own way of expressing their ideas, but within the stylistic context and with absolute fidelity to the original intentions of the composer.

I have been amazed to observe the significant changes in the works being studied even during the course of one lesson with her. And it is even more inspiring to see the developments in individuals after an absence of a week, a month, or even a year or so.

There is one absolute constant in all this and that is Ruth's dedication, enthusiasm, warmth and commitment to her students and her ability to continue to give and give for hours at a time. A typical day at the Royal College, for example, begins at 10am (after being driven up from the farm by Ross) and ends hours later, without this warmth and commitment waning. Her stamina is awe-inspiring. I, a mere observer, may be seriously flagging, while Ruth is still enthusiastically and buoyantly giving of herself, her knowledge and her direction to her students.

Very humorous things happen too…it is not all intense and serious. Once, for example, when I was sitting in on a lesson at the Royal College of Music, a beautiful Fauré work was interrupted by the very loud, unmistakable theme from *Dr Who*! We rushed to the windows to find the irrepressible Nigel Kennedy appropriately dressed and doing a passable 'Doctor' act whilst going beserk on his violin, with the requisite navy blue telephone box, plumes of billowing smoke and other essential ingredients, including a rent-a-crowd, miles of cables and BBC cameras on the steps at the back of the Albert Hall. Because Ruth's room offered the best vantage point, it quickly filled with students and staff. This apparently was a promotion for a soon-to-commence new Proms Season. Then, as quickly as it had happened, it all disappeared, no doubt an act to be repeated in various other parts of London that day.

……………………………..

As I look back over my years of these wonderful musical experiences with Ruth, in my mind it becomes a veritable kaleidoscope of colour. At this stage in my life it is a joy to see these beautiful young faces and minds, absorbing the direction given to them by this great teacher. This generous artist and pedagogue, whose only aim is to pass on the legacy of the legendary Arrau, as well as the benefit of her own long years of experience, does this with spirit and love.

There are just too many to recall but to name just a few who have moved and inspired me: Irish student, Cliodna Shanahan, French student Emmanuel Despax, Japanese students Miho Kawashima and Tomoka Shigeno, South Korean Ji-Ae Ahn, Malaysian Rosalind Phang, English Melissa Gore, Japanese May Kezuka, Portuguese Joao da Camara, and a young English girl, Ursula Perks.

....

From Emmanuel Despax:
Winner of the Royal College of Music's coveted Tagore Gold Medal presented to him by HRH Prince Charles.

....

When I was thirteen my parents divorced and it was decided that it would be best for me to be sent away from France for a year...just to remove me from the situation. Because I was good (they thought) at the piano, and for an opportunity to learn the language, they sent me for consideration to the Yehudi Menuhin School in England. It was a rather terrifying prospect to find myself here without the language.

I was given an initial audition by Ruth Nye, for whom I played Ravel quite badly I think. There was something about this though. I didn't speak a word of English, but somehow we clicked immediately. She managed to convey to me what she wanted and I was able to respond. I think it was probably the luckiest day of my life.

I had no idea myself if I had any talent. I had just been sent there. But she saw something in me I didn't even know about myself. That is one of her great strengths. She can see the raw thing and whether it can be harvested or not.

I used to practise about twenty minutes a day (well, maybe that's exaggeration, but not much!). When she told me I was going to have to practise three or four hours a day, I thought she must be quite mad! She soon made me realise she meant what she had said. I was afraid of her and yet utterly captivated by her.

I went for my first holiday back home to France and had a real holiday. She had armed me with loads of work and I didn't do any of it properly. I was so ashamed when I returned I could hardly look at her. It's not so much that she was very angry with me... she just managed to convey through her looks that she was very disappointed in me, and I was so ashamed. I vowed never to do this again (and over the years we have laughed about this when I say that that holiday at home was the last proper holiday I ever had!).

Ruth's 8am Technique Classes:

I am just not a morning type. I can practise late into the night, but oh it is so difficult to get going early in the mornings! But gradually I learnt that this was a fantastic class, looking at every possible aspect of technique, which of course is a different problem for every individual. She 'sussed' out every possible kind of technical problem and then made us create our own ways to find solutions to them. It was different for everyone. She wanted us to watch others dealing with their own technical problems and how to overcome them. She is so acute, so specific in her teaching. She reaches the very core of every problem. Yet in doing so, she rarely touched the piano; just sometimes she would come to the piano and say, "Put your hand over mine. Can you feel what I am doing here?"

It was two years before I actually heard Ruth play. It was wonderful watching her hands when she played. She was playing late Liszt and I was absolutely bowled over by her interpretive skill and that wonderful sound she produced, and how she produced it – just as she always used to tell us.

When I was about fourteen I stayed at the farm for three days and during that time I was to learn the Scriabin D# minor Study. She said she was going to teach me how to learn – the Scriabin was a completely new language for me. Under her direction I worked like mad for those three days. She taught me how to use my brain, told me I must never ever waste my time at the piano practising automatically. "Your brain must be active...constantly analysing...why this? Why that?"

I have heard Ruth teach the same works to different students and am always amazed that she says different things to different ones. But I have come to realise that that is actually one of her strengths. She just finds the right words to trigger their individual imaginations...different for everyone.

Once you have the stylistic tradition of the composer, the period and everything on the score, then there is space for her to lead you to see what the symbols actually mean. She finds the right words to help you find the meaning yourself. To me, there are two categories of indifferent teachers: in the first category are those who don't think past the physical layer of what's on the score and don't focus on meaning (eg. so long as you play an accented note louder than the surrounding ones, they are quite happy but they don't talk about why the accent is there, what sort of sound, mood, colour lies behind it). A teacher is not actually there to remind you of what is on the page...that is really the job of the 'good student'...but rather to try to make sense of these symbols together with the student, in a way that fulfils both the tradition and period of that particular composer as well as the individuality and imaginative power of the student. A lot of people do one or the other...they are either too correct, cold and intellectual, or disregard the composer entirely and feel free to change whatever dynamic or phrasing as they see fit. I remember hearing Arrau saying in an interview that only when a perfect symbiosis of these two things was achieved could you really have true interpretation.

In the second category they do think past the physical layer of what's on the score but don't encourage the student's individuality to blossom. Instead they fill up the small space left with their own ideas rather than leaving it blank for the student's own imaginative power...they make little clones of themselves.

It was two years before I knew she had studied with Arrau. I was told by Bobby Chen after I told him about a wonderful recording of Arrau's I had been listening to. Ruth is a terribly modest person: she never talked about herself and what she had done. This is something so rare in today's music world. So many top-line teachers would have made so much of that. I know her dear friend Terry had to coax her for a long time to do the lectures about her time with Arrau.

Ruth has led me to consider more carefully all these aspects and so many more. She is an absolutely wonderful teacher and mentor for an artist."

....

THE PIANO MAN

At the foot of the Dolomites, about an hour north of Venice, is the small town of Sacile. Nearby there is a quite small forest of very tall straight spruces which were planted hundreds of years ago to provide timber for the masts of early sailing ships. The trees grow closely together, very slowly, and incredibly straight and tall as they reach up to the sun. It was these special straight spruce trees, which convinced Paolo Fazioli that, if they provided the timber for the early violin makers of the famous Cremona school, there was no good reason why this timber could not be used to make the soundboard of a piano.

Paolo Fazioli has a background as a pianist and also as an engineer; the family business was furniture making. He always knew he wanted to create a different sound from the existing concert pianos...a new character. In 1981 he started.

Nikolai Demidenko speaks enthusiastically about this man and his pianos. "Because of its touch, clarity and evenness, it rivals the great Steinway, and it has something else...a purity and quality of tone which set it apart." He was absolutely mesmerised when he first played one of Paolo's pianos in Terry Lewis's showroom in London. He has owned a Fazioli since 2000 and says he is "in love", that it is, "his mistress".

Paolo Fazioli is obsessed by every single detail of the construction of his pianos. No piano is permitted to leave the Fazioli factory in Sacile until Paolo has played it. He knows exactly what he is looking for. He says he is not in rivalry with other piano makers, but that he just wants a piano to have the sound and quality exactly as he himself wants it to be. This is what has happened. There is an ever increasing number of concert pianists now who are demanding Fazioli pianos. Ruth Nye was one of the first pianists in England to own one.

The Fazioli factory is not like a factory at all: there is a calm stillness. With everyone absolutely intent upon some minute, labour-intensive task, it is more like a church or a library. It seems everyone there is working more at a hobby than at a job. There is total dedication to the task in hand.

In a BBC radio programme Bryce Morrison, the music journalist, said that it was unrealistic not to talk about competition, whether one intends it or not. "Piano manufacturers all over the world are watching Fazioli, and understandably the shift towards this piano by concert artists fills them with a certain unease. Demidenko says, "Most piano-makers consciously or unconsciously try to imitate the Steinway sound. The Fazioli is different." Demidenko is a convert to the Fazioli, but still acknowledges the Steinways' empirical knowledge of centuries, which produces mostly very good pianos. "Paolo Fazioli has used this knowledge but has combined it with science to produce the hitherto unknown possibilities of a piano's quality of sound."

One of the most important differences is in the Duplex scale involved. This principle was invented by Erard and eventually patented by Steinway. Fazioli made it much more specific by using a little moveable bronze bridge which enables the harmonic to be tuned in relation to the note played...a very labour-intensive job but the result is worth the effort. The upper register of his pianos is bright and brilliant in sound and the clarity of the very lowest bass notes so clear. The last three notes on almost every piano have a very unclear pitch...not so on a Fazioli. Another quality, which is extraordinary is that the level of softness achievable is much greater. On most pianos there is a point in pianissimo below which the action doesn't work at all, and concert pianists must be on the alert for this. The Fazioli permits a much wider range from enormous fortes to the very softest sound imaginable...and always remaining warm and rich in quality. It seems you can do anything you wish on this marvellous instrument.

The timber used is the most important factor..."The wood propels the sound to the heavens," says Paolo Fazioli. He also thinks the colours which can be created on his pianos are exceptional.

When asked if he has reached perfection, his ultimate goal, Paolo laughs. "No...it's very good, yes, we get closer and closer but there is no such thing as perfection."

Demidenko says, "It's Paolo Fazioli's experience of life. He has answers to questions we have not yet asked. He is a genius."

....

Paolo Fazioli first met Ruth in 1999. It was a cold, early autumn when she visited Sacile with Nikolai Demidenko, Artur Pizarro and Terry Lewis.

Shortly after Terry began to represent Paolo in the UK the time came to select a concert grand. This piano was to be used for hire. He says...

At that time I was working closely with two major pianists, Nikolai Demidenko, whom I met through Ruth, and Artur Pizarro, winner of the Leeds Piano Competition. These pianists are both remarkable but both like different things in a piano. My problem was that I was only able to have one piano, so how was I to keep both of them happy? The solution...take them both to select the piano! I invited Ruth to join us. We all agreed on the choice of piano within 30 minutes and the boys spent the rest of the available time 'duelling' at the keyboard. One would start playing a concerto and the other would come in with the orchestral part and then they would suddenly switch roles without notice! This went on and on, and for us lesser mortals was wonderful, but Ruthie soon tired of the testosterone and wandered off around the factory.

After some time I went looking and found her in one of the 'voicing' rooms where the pianos are finished off before leaving the factory. She was playing when I went in and found her visibly moved...the reason she explained was that this particular piano was the best she had ever played. Paolo Fazioli had followed shortly behind me and seeing her like this wanted to know what was wrong. Ruth explained and then asked if the piano was available for sale. The trouble was that the piano was already 'earmarked' for a dealer in America. Paolo left the room and a few minutes later returned to announce that his pianos are for pianists who love them and he couldn't live with himself if Ruth didn't get this particular one. He had phoned the dealer in America, and explained the situation, he generously agreed to wait for the next one. Paolo Fazioli is a very special person.

Paolo Fazioli says:

She had impressed me by being a pupil of the great Claudio Arrau, to my mind the most important pianist of the century. And her playing, her sound, her entire approach to the instrument, I loved. She has such refinement, not only of her personality, but also of her playing. Such refinement, such a beautiful cultivated approach, and such a wonderful quality of sound she produces. I realised that for me, this is the quality of sound I want…what I want to be produced on my instrument…this making of one body with the instrument. The love and respect for the instrument. This connection. It is her kind of sound for which I create my instruments.

There is a lovely story about how the delivery was all set up at Longfrey Farm between Ross Nye, Paolo Fazioli and Terry Lewis without Ruth's knowledge, a whole week ahead of the expected date. When she returned from a day's teaching there it was! It is not difficult to imagine the joy. And there it sits today with its companion, the Steinway. Ruth uses the Steinway for teaching and the Fazioli for her own playing. Just sometimes the young concert artists are permitted to perform on it.

Paolo and Ruth both addressed a Symposium of piano technicians in Bristol. Before returning to Sacile he spent some time at Longfrey, where he enjoyed very much being out in the summer sunshine. "Ruth, this is just Paradise." He was fascinated to hear more of the Claudio Arrau story. "This is so marvellous…it needs to be written down!" he told them. It was also an opportunity for him to play both pianos and to make his own comparisons. "I don't say, of course, which is superior," he laughs.

ROSS NYE

There is an extremely important person in the story of Ruth Nye and that is her husband of over 50 years, Ross Nye.

Ross Nye is tall, distinguished looking, a still very physical man and it is almost impossible to believe he is now well into his eighties. He is friendly, warm, but also rather commanding in his manner, a man who has obviously spent his life in the driving seat as it were...the man in charge. He has encountered some health setbacks over more recent years, but with his determination and having had a long lifetime of necessary fitness, has used that determination to overcome it all. He no longer actively runs the stables (leaving most of the hands-on stuff to daughter Kirsty); he is highly respected in London, the county of Surrey, and in England's horse world. He is also extremely protective of the love of his life. At this stage of their life together, Ross drives Ruth to the Royal College of Music twice weekly and this enables him to help Kirsty at the stables, and collect Ruth for the drive home. Ross is still very much the family man, loved and respected by their four grandchildren. In 2009, he and Kirsty took her two sons to the Outback of Queensland, about which he had told them so much over the years. When one thinks about it, what a different kind of life he has had through this marriage to the once brilliant concert pianist and now eminent teacher, from his early years in the Queensland Outback!

In 2002, BBC Radio Four made a programme about this unusual combination, the musician and the horseman. Produced by Bill Lloyd and played on September 9th it is really wonderful, and one of a small series called "The Musical Side of the Family". One of the other families was that of Artur Rubenstein, so you can readily see the company it kept. Ross was interviewed at Longfrey, and simply talked...no rehearsal of any kind... just a natural review of his life experiences and how he came to meet and marry Ruth. He has a wonderful voice and a natural delivery. He claimed there was a great deal in common between teaching a piano student and teaching a young rider...that *'gentling'*, patience and encouragement are needed in both cases.

He spoke of his father, Dr 'Bill' Nye, a specialist physician, who founded the first general hospital in North Queensland and introduced the use of X-rays. His mother came from a pioneering family: she was an Atherton of the Atherton Tableland connection and had been an intrepid horse woman who rode over large areas of the Queensland outback mustering cattle. Ross was drawn to the heritage of his mother's sense of adventure and love of, and knowledge of horses. So, after completing his secondary education, he became a jackeroo...that is, a young man who goes to work to learn on sheep and cattle stations. The money was very poor, about 34 shillings a week. This could be supplemented if you could catch a wild pig, which were a menace on these stations, and for which you were paid an extra few shillings. Everything of course was done whilst riding at a fast speed, and the stories he tells along these lines are breathtaking.

After this experience he and his brother leased a vast tract of land in what he calls the '*real*' outback of North Queensland. He speaks of the aborigines, whose skills he respected so much, who would help them track and find their wild cattle, and whose sharp eyes detected what others could not see. He speaks of his horror at the mal-treatment of horses during the '*breaking in*' process, which he had witnessed since his childhood and which had made him vow that when his time came to do so, he would '*gentle*' a horse, never break one in. He speaks lovingly of these "great gentle four-legged creatures who will do anything we want within reason and who are gregarious by nature ... who love company." He explains how these wild creatures of the Outback have never seen or smelt a human being, and how one must seemingly ignore them, and gently, and gradually gain their confidence. It is in these stories that we find the real Ross Nye.

....

Ross' meeting Ruth, and their early married life in Australia and the significant move to New York has already been told in an earlier chapter.

....

Ross had the deepest respect and affection for Claudio Arrau, and Arrau equally enjoyed Ross' company.

He remembers a week they spent with the Arraus on their property in Vermont. Walking around the estate with the maestro, he saw how he loved his gardens but could not actively do anything himself...he didn't quite know how. He would say, "Ross dear, would you cut this branch for me?" or "Ross dear, would you do this for me? I can't do it myself. I wish I knew how. But I can only play the piano." To which Ross would answer, "But maestro, look how you play the piano!" He remembers the practical Ruth Arrau saying, "For goodness sake, Claudie, don't pretend you can peel that apple in front of Ruthie and Ross. Here...give it to me!"

Ross Nye felt that Arrau was in many ways like a child...that he always needed someone to look after him, to do things for him. This is true of so many great artists, especially those who had come from being child prodigies. He had a secure family life though and three children, and dogs, so there was all that kind of necessary normality in his life and his wife, Ruth, was the amazing, warm and wonderful woman who facilitated it all.

In England on one occasion came a telephone call from Arrau – "Ross dear, I need some help. Could you drive me to Liverpool and then to Manchester for my concerts?" (two concerts in three days!) But what he didn't say was, "and may we visit my tailor (in

London) in between the concerts?" It was November and very foggy (the old pea-souper type), with no motorways in the mid sixties, so the return at night to Manchester was quite scary for Ross. He (Arrau) was fascinated by the 'cats' eyes' on the roads and thoroughly enjoyed an evening meal at a transport cafe! As Ross says it was something like driving from A to B via Z.

At the stables themselves, Claudio Arrau was so interested in the horses. He never touched them ...oh no...but he wanted to look at them, and he would breathe in delight, "Oh Ross dear, isn't he strong...isn't he sweet...isn't he a beauty!" depending on which horse it was. It was a genuine love he had for the horses as he did for all animals. And can you believe it, one of his sons was actually a rodeo rider on the American circuit, which means he must have been a top class rider – that is extraordinary!

Ross concludes by saying, "I have always had a great love of music, and through my Ruthie I have learned and appreciated so much more.

"I am often asked if I ever regret the steps I have taken and the great changes I made in my life all those years ago. And I can honestly say, 'No I certainly don't. And I consider myself to be one very lucky boy to have married Ruth, and long may it continue.'"

....

I am sure the reader feels, as I have always done, that this is one very special man.

FORTY YEARS !

In 2005 I was fortunate enough to be able to attend the Forty Year Birthday Party of the Ross Nye Stables in Bathurst Mews. It was a delightful occasion with decorations across the Mews, big Happy Birthday notices, and tables with food and drinks set up. I had just flown in from Australia, so it was great to be able to catch up again with my very dear friends and their families and to catch up also with several other guests I knew.

Then in 2008 there was another big celebration here...the Fortieth anniversary of "Horsemen's Sunday" on September 23rd. The event is a very special one in the calendar of St John's Church on the north side of Hyde Park. The riders and horses gather nearby and at the stroke of 12 the procession begins, led by the Vicar on horseback. When all the horses are settled in the crescent in front of the church, the service begins.

There were hymns and prayers for the safety of riders everywhere, and Ross made a moving speech about how he felt that in this time of enormous commercial concentration and the rush and pace of life, it had been very special for him to be able to offer something calmer, with more chance of reflection, less of a commercial aspect, in the close confines of this busy London city, but with the glorious expanses of Hyde Park...more like the country...so close by.

All coachmen, totters and riders received a rosette and were introduced to the large crowd.

Kirsty Anthony spoke:

I want to pay tribute to a great man: my father. He started this Hyde Park Horsemen's Sunday in 1968 because he wanted to make the occasion possible for horses and riders who couldn't get to the larger service at Epsom Racecourse. He also wanted to raise awareness of the difficulties being faced by the stables in our area. But more than that, he just thought, Why Not? And to me this characterises my father. He always sees the answers rather than the problems; he always sees the potential rather than the limitations. This is why he had come all the way across the world with his wife and two small children all those years ago when so many others would have thought the difficulties involved would have been too great.

I want to take this opportunity to thank him for what he has done for so many people: this Church Service, developing riding in Central London, his support and assistance for Riding for the Disabled and so much more. The list is too long to relate here. His is the first urban stable to have been granted British Horse Society Approval, the first Pony Club branch to be based in a commercial stable, the Order of Merit he received from the BHS, the Silver Award from the Pony Club, the Long Service awards from the RDA to name just a few of the awards to Ross Nye.

I would like to acknowledge his constant enthusiasm and his incredibly hard work over so many years...for example, not many people would undertake to organise a large event like this at the age of eighty...but this is my father. I thank him for the positive impact, which he has had on so many people because of his personality, his vision, his self-belief, and his fundamental love of horses, and for his teaching of that love to all of us.

....

About eighty horses and riders take part in this service each year.

CEREMONIAL

The Brits do ceremonial so well, don't they!

Ruth Nye was awarded an MBE (Member of the British Empire) for her services to Music Education in the Queen's Birthday Honours List of 2007, which was presented to her on October the 25th.

In a Buckingham Palace DVD, 'Path of Honour', one sees the recipients and their guests arriving, ascending the great marble palace staircase, strolling in the beautiful reception rooms and admiring the priceless collection of art, magnificent sights which will be remembered. The guests enter the ballroom to take their seats, and the recipients are briefed in a charmingly relaxed manner regarding the particular protocol of the coming ceremony by a palace official. They are a mixed group of men and women from various fields, some extremely elegantly dressed, who chat in a waiting room which would be one of very few in the world where such a superb display of art can be viewed. 'The ceremony will take place in the ballroom at 11am. Your name will be called and Forward you go!' and similar instructions, as they are walked through the procedures. The atmosphere is a combined one of relaxation and anticipation. Stuffy formality is definitely out, but naturally a certain propriety needs to be observed.

The Buckingham Palace Ballroom is not used as such any more. It is merely the largest room in the palace, 122 ft long and 60 ft wide, the scene of state banquets, investitures and other state occasions. It is a most beautiful and richly decorated salon.

All stand as HRH Prince Charles and his Household enter. The band plays the national anthem and then he himself invites them, "Ladies and Gentlemen please be seated."

Names are called, and the recipients come forward individually to receive their awards from the Prince, men bowing slightly and the women a brief curtsey before and after investiture. They had been urged by the protocol officer beforehand to remember that each was to be a short but *two-way* conversation, so "please engage!" One notices that Ruth engages delightfully with Prince Charles and their brief smiling conversation is obviously a mutually enjoyable one.

More Ceremonial was to happen very soon.

In April 2008, Ruth Nye MBE was created a Fellow of the Royal College of Music (FRCM), joining the ranks of many distinguished musicians of history before her.

Once again the ceremony was a colourful and dignified affair. The presentations were made in the RCM's Britten Theatre followed by a reception in the beautiful setting of the concert hall. Of course, this time the recipients of this award were very few indeed.

Ruth looked wonderfully relaxed in her academic dress as a speech outlining her history and the reasons for this honouring of her as a distinguished professor was read, and again she chatted in a relaxed way with HRH Prince Charles, the President of the College, who bestowed the symbol of the Fellowship upon her.

The Prince and his Household mingled with the guests for a short while at a reception afterwards and later we all attended a delightful supper party in the Kensington home of Terry Lewis where Ruth was immersed in the warmth of all those who love her dearly.

When I asked her some time later which of these two honours she valued more, Ruth thought for a while before answering. "Of course receiving the MBE was a great privilege and a great honour for which I am most delighted and grateful. However, the FRCM was as a result of nomination by my Royal College of Music colleagues, and because of this perhaps means even more to me."

CONVERSATIONS
WITH RUTH NYE

In August 2007, after so many visits to Longfrey farm, I am driving there again, but this time with the mutually agreed intention of some recorded interviews with Ruth...to fill in the gaps as it were and as I drove, I mulled over the questions I had prepared.

In what follows, I am attempting to give Ruth's views on various topics, which really are the very essence of her philosophy of teaching. It is by no means a complete version of the eight interviews ...far from it. I have just selected some questions and answers from the total, hoping that these will be of the most interest, and will reinforce the second of Ruth's two public lectures. Ruth and I have a very easy relationship so these interviews, though focused and specific, were conducted in a relaxed manner, with many intervening stories and many laughs.

[In what follows, my questions are in italics; Ruth's answers are in Roman type.]

Martin Krause studied with Liszt in Weimar and he regarded the young Arrau as being another Liszt. But he is reported to have told the young Arrau, "You don't acquire any more technique after the age of twenty." I find this a rather amazing statement, and wonder what you think.

Maybe what Krause meant was that it's too late at the age of twenty to acquire a really full, seemingly easy natural technique. There is no doubt that the earlier I get a student the better, so I can guide this development, towards dealing with the "gymnastics" of the piano...like one of those young Olympic gymnasts. You can build on what has been acquired when young, so long as it has been the right thing, but the earlier this 'right thing' is acquired the better. However, it doesn't stop there: Arrau said to me when he was in his seventies, "You know, dear, as you get older, your muscles get wiser." This is a marvellous idea. Of course the muscles do lose something, but as they do, they compensate with the wisdom acquired over the years, and they say, "I can still do this."

When you studied with Lindsay Biggins, did he talk much about correct technique?

Lindsay rather left it to us, but he knew well the importance of the balance between relaxation and tension when playing and he insisted the technical work was an integral part of daily practice. I believe I always just had an intuitive knowledge of how to do it, but it was Arrau who taught me the principles and the realisation of how to achieve this. When he first heard me play he asked me, "Who taught you to use your arms this way?" and I just said, "Well, no one really...I just do." Lindsay Biggins was wonderful in other ways: he knew particularly, when there was some performance or competition coming up, how to get us to our peak at just the right time...much like a race-horse trainer. So we were lucky in that we had had no actual disadvantages in our early years of learning. You know, when you get a student of eighteen coming to the College there are so often problems to be overcome, even if he/she is a brilliant young performer, and it often takes me about two years to overcome the physical problems which inhibit the creation of beautiful sound and, to be realistic, there is usually a limit to what one can achieve. It is just so much easier if one can lay the technical foundation as young as possible, which probably reinforces Krause's statement in your first question.

Krause made his students practise difficult works at different speeds, in different keys, different styles etc. Do you believe in this approach?

I agree with the different speeds and keys but I am not sure what is meant by different styles. On occasion I have asked a student who is working on the Chopin Etude Op10 No 1 to bring it to me the following week in C sharp Major, using C Major fingering. It is an excellent exercise. Here we have the mental and physical "gymnastics" I speak of.

It is reported that Krause instructed Arrau and others that you should never give a public performance unless you had enormous reserves of power which you would not need in this performance ...that you needed to be able to play the work ten times faster and louder than would be needed. How do you view this?

Well, again, it is a somewhat exaggerated statement! If you are, as it were, right at the edge of the precipice in performance, such that it creates real fear, the audience will know it; you won't get away with it. Fear usually stems from the knowledge that your technique is not quite good enough to cope easily with a certain passage that it is very difficult for you, and this interferes with the interpretation. It destroys that communication; that inspired realisation of the music. You are trying too hard, and it shows. I often find problems when a student does not realise that the correct speed has been reached. Young people, <u>especially</u> perhaps young men, often continue to over-strive, and consequently the musical content is submerged.

Furtwangler wrote in 'Concerning Music' "The moment you have any technical problems in performance, it interferes with the spiritual unity and the music is destroyed." Someone quoted this to Arrau and he is reported to have said that he loved it...that it was absolutely correct. Technique must never be an end in itself.

The wrong kind of tension is created when there is a technical problem in a work being performed. Of course there needs to be a certain amount of tension to be able to perform at all, but it must be controlled tension, not destructive tension, which will badly affect your interpretation. If the problem you have is a technical one, your mind is taken away from the music and your interpretation is stunted.

I so often say to my students: "You must practise technique tirelessly. But the moment it becomes an end in itself it destroys the music. Technique is a very good servant, but must never become your master."

And wherever difficulties with certain passages remain, it is so often the choice of fingering causing the problem. Don't always use the most obvious fingering either; use your imagination: sometimes a change of fingering will totally alter the sound. Choice of fingering is perhaps the single most important decision.

Can you talk a bit about size of hands and fingers?

Adjustments need to be made for both. A large hand has advantages and disadvantages. For example, a large hand needs to make many adjustments, e.g. in playing octaves cleanly. And that person must fold up his hand more in so many instances. I have small hands and Arrau told me he would much prefer to work with a small hand than a large one "because a large one can get lazy" (he was probably boosting my confidence). Someone with small hands needs to be especially courageous to perform more demanding works. But it is so important you don't allow a student with small hands to think they have a problem.

How specifically do you teach trilling? We know there are so many ways to trill, depending on the context within the work.

The action of trilling, it is the smallest possible lateral movement one makes, and you don't want to leave the keys. Stay there and just use your arm and your finger tips. Articulating them unduly is not the way to go. Lifting your fingers right up wastes time, slows the trill. The arm is terribly important when trilling; this lateral movement you have perfected. And of course, every trill must be fast or slow, or increasing or decreasing entirely within the context of the work. And the same with all ornaments: they must fit in with the musical intention. I often urge students to listen to a singer trilling.

So much of Arrau's teaching (apart from his ideas regarding technique) was about interpretation. He was also not averse to painting a programme if a student seemed not to be grasping the correct interpretation of a work. You do this too.

Arrau was so wonderful with his use of literary and emotional imagery. In this way he was able to convey to you, for example, exactly what was needed in a Beethoven sonata. I feel very strongly, however, that the art of the teacher is to put it across in such a way that the student will actually do it himself, that one doesn't spell it out too clearly for them on every occasion. You just need to ease them on to the right track, not do it for them.

My students are encouraged to read very widely, so that they actually have a library of literary ideas, as it were, on which to draw. This wider education is so important to their intellectual as well as to their musical growth.

We know that the Liszt B minor Ballade is based on the 'Leander and Hero' legend. This comes down to us from Liszt to Krause to Arrau. There are many other Liszt works, which have literary bases because he read so widely. But where the composer has not told us, interpretation is even more of a challenge. The composer can't write you a letter! The students are allowed to have various interpretive possibilities themselves of course, but often it won't be a convincing one. I tell them so. If they are a bit miffed about this, I say, "All right. Play it for me again and this time, convince me." Nine times out of ten, after trying something different, they will admit it doesn't work – <u>but that's the important point</u>: the student has worked it out for himself.

That is fascinating. And yes that has always been one of the wonderful things I have observed when sitting in on many of your lessons: your great gift of imagery. And the musically intelligent student (as all yours are) can pick up on this immediately. I have seen it happen so often. But now, tell me: how on earth do you teach the enormous subject of pedalling?

As you well know yourself, we must teach the very basics of pedalling. But beyond that, it is not really something you can actually teach at all. You might suggest some use. But basically, it is all up to the performer's ear. What you do need to teach them is to use their ears properly. And in an exceptionally musical student you find it is an intuitive thing: they are doing it well and imaginatively without even thinking about it. But they have no doubt thought about it long and hard beforehand, and then it just becomes natural for them. What they do need to understand right from the beginning is the types of Pedalling….the half pedal etc. And also about the effect achieved when you put the pedal down before a chord is played; it creates a different kind of resonance altogether: the piano has been "opened up already" as it were – a very useful effect sometimes. You know, once I had a student who attended a master class given by a quite notable musician, and he came back and told me that the person giving this class had questioned his use of the pedal. When he explained he had been using half pedals he had been told there was no such thing: you either put the pedal right down or you don't! I couldn't believe it; just couldn't believe it! It is such a huge topic. Once I said to a student, "Your pedalling isn't bad. You are not doing anything wrong. But it is not *imaginative*." So many just 'blanket' pedal. I coaxed her to find out for herself more imaginative uses, and at the next session, the change in that particular work was amazing. I liked it very much. You see, you really need to let them try to solve problems themselves first before you intervene too much. In this way they grow.

Busoni called the pedal 'The Soul of the piano'. And that's what it is. And you teach the basics, but it has to become homogenous and intuitive. Once I must have thought it all out very clearly for myself…but honestly, when anyone has asked me after a performance what I have been doing with the pedal, I am unable to tell them precisely. I wouldn't have a clue. Someone, for example, once asked me to write in the pedalling I had been using when I had just played the Opus 25, No 7 Etude by Chopin. It was an impossible request. It had become absolutely intuitive for me. I think it always was, actually. And pedalling also depends on the particular piano being used and also the acoustic. I would be very surprised if I always pedalled the same work in the same way. One of my most treasured compliments came from John Dankworth, after I had played a recital at his and Cleo Lane's Wavenden Stable. He said to me, "I wish you hadn't been wearing a long skirt, as I wanted to see what you were doing with your pedals."

So again, what is most important (after the basic principles and techniques of pedalling are known) is to teach them how to use their ears to pedal. You teach them how to listen to themselves. Then to decide what they want, and to consider that all variation of pedalling adds a wide subtlety of colour.

We must be very careful indeed about any use of the pedal when playing Bach. When we want precise articulation, it is better to leave the pedal alone, and if we do use it at all, it must never be obvious (here of course is the matter of *types* of pedal use). But a lot of Bach is such that use of the pedal is actually called for. We need to remember that Bach was a great organist as well and we need to try to recreate the resonance I believe he intended. And where there are really long vocal lines, as in the aria-like long flowing lines of the Second Movement of the Italian Concerto, I feel you cannot just play this absolutely dry with no pedal at all. I know some do, but to me it is not convincing. Bach's compositions can be divided into dance, keyboard and voice, and it is important to remember this and pedal accordingly.

What about pedalling in Scarlatti?

Well, like all of us, I was taught to play Scarlatti without any pedal, and when a young student in Australia, I believed this was the correct way. But years ago, I changed my mind. I thought, "the harpsichord is a resonant instrument, not a powerful instrument, but it is resonant and it certainly, because of this, calls for careful use of the pedal."

And what about with Mozart?

You have to be so careful with Mozart. Arrau told us that Busoni said, "In every Mozart sonata there is an opera trying to get out!" So much of Mozart is about characters, drama, and of course you need to use the pedal. But the use of it must be discreet...you need to know exactly where to pull back...where to concentrate on delicacy and absolute clarity above all. So the choice of pedalling in Mozart becomes even more important. You are playing it on a different instrument: it is not a fortepiano. You can think of it like having a lovely lace blouse. You wouldn't wear this blouse for gardening. The material is strong, but the thread is more delicate. So you wear it only at the appropriate times.

He also had that 'galant' style...in the earlier salon pieces, but not often. Most of his works were quite operatic...dramatic. There is drama in his sonatas and chamber works. The pedal should never blur in Mozart. We should use a 'hidden' pedal for colour – if it is noticeable it is wrong. After all most of Mozart's runs are melodies. I am always bemused when a pianist becomes 'digital' at the sight of a few bars of semiquavers!

Now, let's turn to Chopin. Can you speak a little about Chopin's pedalling?

Chopin was unique. Liszt said, "He was the greatest pedaller who ever lived."

We all know you cannot play Chopin without correct use of the pedal. Sometimes he wrote 'ped, ped, ped' and it doesn't make sense till you realise that what he wanted was the performer to *use* the pedal, but *how to use it* was a matter of personal interpretation. Of course, other times he was more specific. Sometimes he wrote long pedals, when he wanted a long wash of sound. But more often than not, he was depending on the innate knowledge and feeling of the interpreter to use it in such a way to produce the loveliness he wanted. Chopin perhaps gives the pianist the most headaches; he is at times pedantic about his writing of pedal marks. I discover more and more that the use of *'half-pedal'* often produces the effect he was after. So again, it is all about teaching students to use their ears. And to think, and make decisions about the actual kind of sound they want to produce...in Chopin, as with any other composer. With Chopin particularly, they just need to relate to his period and style and to consider the sound of his Pleyel piano.

Now to perhaps the biggest topic of all: the matter of the use of Total Body Weight, and how on earth this can be taught. I know this is what Arrau was all about originally (and the story about the mirrors etc) but Barenboim for example (a great devotee of Arrau) said that you couldn't just adopt part of it...you had to adopt the entire philosophy or leave it alone. I personally sensed he finally didn't feel total conviction regarding this. Could I be right? Do you still? Do you still believe in it 100%?

Yes I do. Absolutely, but I would call it Natural Body Weight. It makes perfect sense. The trouble was that a few of his so-called 'disciples', in the late sixties or early seventies 'got the wrong end of the stick' and thought it was all about playing with arms and not enough importance to the fingers. They were so misguided...so wrong. It was ridiculous really just *how* wrong they were. Arrau had fingers like steel. He could do amazing things with his fingers. But it was his imagination and the way he used it, which helped those fingers to produce the *quality* of the sound which was so special to Arrau. And it is the quality of sound I am most interested in...though naturally, everything else is also of the utmost importance. Without using your body in a certain way, and your imagination, the quality of the sound will not be the same: it will be blocked.

Think about it. The fingers must be strong. It is the first finger joint that holds up the weight of the hand and the arm, while the knuckles which join the finger to the hand must become like butter. This is the aim. There must be no blockage allowed to develop in the wrist. If there is, the arm becomes tense, and shoulders, back...everything...follow. And the quality of the sound is then lost. It is the quality of the sound we are aiming for. If everything else (all the other aspects of technique etc.) is in place, the quality of the sound can be achieved, but only after a considerable period of study with the correct approach to the use of natural body weight. This is what I teach.

I have been told so often that not only the sound of my students is recognisable, but also the <u>way</u> they play.

One member of staff at the Menuhin School was at a concert recently and said to me afterwards, "Not only do I love the sound your students create, but I also enjoy watching the way they use their arms."

The sound starts in your head and imagination then proceeds through your body...your whole body produces it. It has to be absolutely organic. You cannot create barriers. Even the shoes are an important consideration for girls...high heels throw the body off balance, and then everything risks being off balance.

You need to <u>think </u>the sound you want and then use your entire body to produce it. It is possible to change the emotion of the sound just by thinking it, and then doing what is necessary. Thinking it before you play is the most important thing. Of course, it becomes so refined over time, the listener and watcher is not usually aware of what is going on in the body...but it <u>is</u> happening if that particular quality of sound has been produced.

I thought Emmanuel's opening of the Chopin Op 25 no. 11 Etude yesterday was so perfect. I thought that no one in the world could possibly play it better...and then the dramatic contrast which followed! Perfect.

Yes, I too thought that. Of course the adjudicators of the competition may not quite like the opening that way. But tough!...he must remain true to himself. He must play it the way his personal thought and study have led him to think it. The lateral movements of the fast passages were also excellent. Arrau spoke of "waves of sound", and Emmanuel knows all about this and is able to produce it when he wishes.

It is really nothing to do with finger-tips the way most people teach that concept. Thinking about the finger-tips needs to be much more analytic. You encourage them to think of their finger-tips as 'needle points' or as being 'fat and thick' etc., as the music demands. That works much better. The sound can be altered so amazingly just by thinking it the right way.

Let's talk about Legato. How do you teach it? I know Arrau was so strong on the topic of legato playing.

You first have to accept that the piano is not a legato instrument...not like a violin or cello for instance. It is a percussive instrument, but you can make it so many things...so many different things, if you have the skill. We are so lucky to have such a wonderful instrument. Legato is 50% illusion and 50% fact. Chopin told his students to go and listen to singers to understand about legato. Arrau taught it was all about *weight-shifting*. You have to shift the weight from one finger to another...through your hands. It is not merely about playing one note after another without a break. And pedalling will not create legato! It only hangs on to the sound you make. It is about the weight you need to shift in order to create a truly legato sound. When you think about it, with the hammer action, and the arrangement of the keys of the piano, to play absolute legato seems impossible. But it *is* possible to do it when you know exactly how, and therein lies the illusion. One must leave a note with 'legato care'. Often pianists don't care how they leave a note!

Over my many years of teaching I have come to the conclusion that what I teach is more a *philosophy* of playing than any method. You pass on the basics necessary, but then each person must be allowed to adapt them for himself. You must never inhibit this freedom (unless of course, they are entirely on the wrong track). It must be sinuous, and if it is not sinuous, it is wrong. Of course some things have to be adapted because of body size, hand size etc.,...it cannot be absolutely the same for everyone. But the basic philosophy is set in stone. You are not going to get the quality of sound you are aiming for if they don't follow these important principles. And finally they do. Watch them before the start of any performance: they are thinking; it is surging up inside them...and then they commence. And that's what it's all about. So many put down the first notes without 100% care and thought.

So, they have been taught about the ways of achieving things, and then they mould it to their own personalities. You can think of it as a kind of plasticine that can be moulded into shape. It is malleable...but the philosophy and principles remain cast in stone.

Well, this is the way you teach. This is why you are so revered as a teacher. This philosophy of yours produces results. We hear it in the sound.

I always say to them, "Don't attack the piano. Leave the piano some dignity. You must coax the instrument, never bully it."

That's the most wonderful expression: leave the piano some dignity. You know, someone like myself is often searching for a word to describe a performance I have not enjoyed so much. 'Bullying' is such a good one. I have so often sat through a brilliant artist's performance and have been left cold. I appreciate it has been a technically brilliant performance, but it has not drawn me in. And if it hasn't drawn me in emotionally, I am left cold. This seems to happen more as I get older. Maybe it's because I know more about it. Maybe, with age, I am more discerning. All I know is that so often despite the obvious brilliance of a performance, there is something happening which spoils it for me. And your word 'bullying' is maybe what I need in these circumstances.

Yes, I know what you mean. And there is so much performance like that today.

Now, tell me how you deal with the prodigy situation. This is surely another large topic.

We encounter it all the time at the Menuhin School. So many of them, having been accepted from all parts of the world, *are* real prodigies. Our Director of Music, Malcolm Singer, whom you know, has said so often, "Here we are a school for children with special needs." This is so true. He is not talking about their musical needs; that's obvious. He is talking about the personal needs their musical brilliance has actually created for them. Our important task is to see that they are treated as normally as possible. They need normality in their lives. And there is very good Pastoral Care at the school too. One important thing they must learn is self-discipline. Of course, they know that they are special musically, or they wouldn't be there at all. But we go to some lengths to try to minimise this as much as possible; they are just all the same. All this is normal…they are all treated the same way, and must abide by the same rules and keep to set rosters etc. This is so important. We aim to try to keep some very important balance in their young lives. It is much discussed by all of us with the great responsibility of looking after and teaching these very special children and nurturing them, so that their growth is wholesome and not only confined to music. We aim to produce really well-balanced young people, as well as exceptional musicians.

How many hours a day did you practise when you were seriously on the performing circuit?

I generally practised about six hours.

Arrau said the hands should never become tired, didn't he? The body should never become tired. This depends on using the body correctly. Only the brain can become tired after many hours of practice. Do you subscribe to this?

121

Yes, of course. But you must exercise properly as well. Sport is compulsory at the School. They do swimming, aerobics, cross country hikes, and there are tennis and soccer offered too. I don't like mine to play tennis...it is too much of a strain for the wrists. (Yes, I can see you are amazed!) I also don't like the soccer, because they can get hurt, and some of them do. Fast walking over quite long distances, and swimming are probably the best exercises of all for students.

Is it easy, in an audition, to see who is going to do well at the School and who has less potential?

This is interesting. Sometimes you *think*, there is something special. And yet, there are others, who play well, full of enthusiasm and confidence, but you don't see the same potential. It is a matter of having had many years of experience.

The repeated 4th fingers in Chopin you have described. Surely that is a glissando?

No...it's a succession of notes played with the 4th finger. It is like a sensuous glissando without being one. You'll find it particularly in very melodic passages of the Nocturnes. It feels so wonderful when you adhere to his fingering.

Repeated notes. We were taught to play them with rapidly changing fingers (321 etc.). But there are other ways, aren't there?

It depends on the work concerned...the type of repeat needed. You can do it rapidly using one finger only or with two, or with three or four. But you must first find out what is best for you, and what is best within the context of the work. A good example is the beginning of 'Scarbo': some change fingers, others don't.

Fear. Anxiety. We know this is negative.

Arrau always said that fear can spoil an entire performance. It is of course true. And if you make an issue of a student's mistake in performance you will possibly cause real damage. There is not a performing artist anywhere in the world who will not occasionally make mistakes on the concert platform or has a slight memory lapse. The great skill is in the speed of recovery so it won't be noticed. I tell my young performing artists that you must always have a spot in your brain for any emergency. You have perfected your technique, you know the work so well, you have thought about every aspect of it, so that when you go out to perform it, you are doing so with entire confidence and you are not thinking about this 'Red Alert'. But if something should happen...if you should have a slight memory lapse, the Red Button comes on, and you know how to get out of it without break-down. There is a great difference between Nerves and Anxiety. Anxiety can be destructive. But we are all nervous before performance. Nerves are actually necessary in order to be able to give a vital performance. But the nerves need to be controllable. This is where successful performers have it. There have been unfortunately some excellent performers who simply have been unable to cope with the extraordinary level of uncontrollable nerves before public performance and have therefore decided to abandon any idea of a public career...even though the artistic ability was there in full.

Another very important consideration. You must *want* to get out there and perform. You must have that desire. You are a 'performer'...with all this word connotes. You perform! It has to be a 'magnificent obsession'!

Are you nervous when your students are performing?

No. Not really. I always tell them, and myself, "The sun will still come up tomorrow no matter what happens tonight." After all these years and all these performing young artists of mine, if I became nervous, I would never have been able to continue.

How do you advise your young performing artists how to cope with conductors if they are being difficult?

Arrau was always exceedingly polite, and was often horrified by the way some conductors behaved towards him when he was young. But he knew what he wanted...he knew what was correct. But he was always so professional, and so immensely polite himself even when his career was very well established. He would never say anything the orchestra could hear. He would leave the piano and go up and talk quietly with the conductor, always careful to leave the conductor his dignity. When I was young and performing a lot, I was playing for the ABC in Australia, Beethoven's 1st and 3rd concertos (in 4 concerts) conducted by Sir Malcolm Sargent. He was so kind, and asked me to come and see him the day before the first concert to go through the scores with him and to tell him what I wanted. After the first performance in Melbourne, the car dropped him off first at his hotel and he didn't go straight up the stairs. He stayed there, hand on heart, till we were out of sight.

But for my pianists today, I have to tell them to be very polite, but to show exactly what they want and why. And make sure it is well understood.

Barenboim said that Arrau had the most remarkable sound...unlike anyone else's. And that for him, there were two sides to it. One, a thick orchestral type of sound, and the other a disembodied mysterious one, which was electrifying. Both types were just wonderful.

He also had the most utter clarity and superb imagination. He said, "You have to believe you can do it. You have to have the equipment to do it. Then you have to know you can do it. And then you do it."

Fidelity to the score. I know that Arrau was so strong about this...the composer's intentions above all else. And I know you are too.

Yes, I am extremely concerned about the works being played exactly according to the composer's intentions, and insist upon use of the Urtext. You may add your own interpretation once you know the work 100% from the original score. What Arrau would never allow was any cheating …means used (different hands etc.) which made a passage easier to play. Everything was written the way it was for a reason. Removing the technical difficulty can so often destroy the quality of emotion intended, because the inner tension is removed. And it can also lead to different problems. I watch out for and emphasise this when I see it happening. You have a responsibility to play what the composer intended. I feel very strongly about this.

Philip Lorenz assisted Arrau when he undertook the enormous task of a new edition of the Beethoven Sonatas for Peters. Do you like it?

In this edition, Arrau put some of his fingerings and other markings in brackets. I always told him that I wished he had done an accompanying booklet to go with this edition. He used to say he would, but it never happened. Philip Lorenz and he were very close. Arrau was a father figure to Philip.

Tell me about the big Bonn Masterclasses to mark the Beethoven Bi-Centennial in September, 1970.

With his worldwide Beethoven reputation Arrau was the obvious choice to give these Master classes. My brother Ron and I were among the few participants. Ron played the Opus 101 and I played the 'Eroica Variations'. At the conclusion of this series, there was to be a final concert in Bonn's largest concert hall which was to be broadcast over German Radio and I was among those chosen to play the 'Eroica'. But Arrau had become ill, and Ruth Arrau had flown over to be with him. So people thought the concert might be cancelled. But no, it was to go ahead, although we thought at the time, without his presence. I remember walking on to the stage to play and not really noticing the large audience. It went well, and as I was bowing and acknowledging the audience afterwards, there he was in the front row, applauding and smiling widely. I remember thinking I was so glad I had not noticed him before I had commenced playing!

Are there any other things you can say about your teaching today?

Well there is one final thing I want to state emphatically. I feel very strongly about it. I absolutely cannot tolerate destructive teaching. It is so easy for a teacher to build himself up by putting a student down. It is the easiest kind of teaching…but the very worst. Of course this is not to say I am not sometimes very displeased with a student when he or she has not done what I regard as being adequate preparation and I then tell them so very emphatically. I tell them that if there are time constraints or other problems they must tell me, not try to cover up. But I emphasise it is their responsibility. Unless there is a real problem they must *never* come in for their lessons unprepared. But usually they are very good. They say, "It's when she goes very quiet that you really need to worry"!

Ruth, you don't find it all too tiring?

Well of course I can become tired sometimes. Who doesn't? But you know, when I get into a lesson, I lose any trace of that and the enthusiasm takes over. It creates its own kind of buoyancy. And you would agree, I am sure, that even where the talent is limited, if you help a person with their talent, you help to make them a better person. Their personality blossoms. I feel great satisfaction in seeing this happening. It is a different kind of satisfaction to watching the successes of the very gifted ones. But it is also very enriching.

(A thought of my own): This is so much of what Ruth Nye is all about. It speaks of her total humanity, both as a teacher and as a human being.

....

126

CONCLUSION

How to sum up my experiences and my relationship with Ruth Nye presents me with a considerable challenge. I offer her this small work I have put together as my tribute to a most wonderful musician and extraordinary human being, and with all my love. Her story is one I personally find remarkable and I see myself just as something of a conduit in this regard. It is a story that deserves to be told.

Since our meeting all those years ago, I know with absolute conviction that she made an enormous difference in my life. She led me down so many new avenues, filled me with new inspiration, gave me new insights, and has given me so much of herself, that mere words can never be adequate repayment. But words are all I have.

Ruth's generosity of spirit as well as in kind, has been monumental and I and all those associated with her have been very privileged recipients. I believe she is a truly unique musical personality and a visionary teacher and communicator, as witnessed by so many, and publicly acknowledged by Crown and Peers. She is also possessed of a very strong spirituality, which has nothing at all to do with religion. I continue to marvel at all she accomplishes without seeming to flag as each year passes. She remains an incredibly generous, extremely practical, delightfully humorous, a laughing wise and steadfast being, with a love of life and a love of knowledge. It might be argued that she is driven … I wouldn't absolutely disagree. Underneath that gentle exterior she can be tough when necessary. She is determined, she can be stubborn, she wouldn't deny that she might sometimes be a touch competitive, and she somehow always manages to get people to do what she wants. This is an art form, which has brought valuable rewards, not just for herself, but for all those she strives to assist.

Over the years she has taken no time out to recharge her own batteries unless illness has absolutely forced it, and she never dwells on any misfortune. She remains happy doing what she does, and continues to do so magnificently. Who could argue with that?

Ruth Nye loves hugely and loves to be loved. In fact, I feel bound to observe that this delightfully feminine sparkling woman maybe sparkles even more in the admiring company of men! She loves to be surrounded by people, by family and good friends, to party, to reminisce, to experience beauty of every kind. Ruth is a 'people person' in the best possible sense.

In a world where broken marriages abound, her enduringly strong and loving partnership with her husband of so many years is a reassuring joy to observe.

She is my wise counsellor, my musical mentor, and above all, my very dear and loyal friend.

Circa 1950

With Kirsten and Lisa circa 1963.

Circa 1960

CONCERTO REPERTOIRE includes :

BACH—F minor.

MOZART—D minor (K.466).
 B flat major (K.450).
 D major (K.537) Coronation.
 C minor (K.491).

BEETHOVEN—No. 1 in C major.
 No. 2 in B flat major.
 No. 3 in C minor.
 No. 4 in G major.

MENDELSSOHN—G minor.

GRIEG—A minor.

CHOPIN—F minor.

LISZT—A major.
 Totentanz.

SCHUMANN—A minor

WEBER—Konzertstücke.

CESAR FRANCK—Symphonic Variations

TSCHAIKOWSKY—G major.

RACHMANINOFF—Variations on a Theme of Pag

DOHNANYI—Variations on a Nursery Song.

HINDEMITH—Four Temperaments.

KABALEVSKY—No. 2 in G minor.

PROKOFIEV—No. 3 in C major.

STRAVINSKY—Capriccio

Enquiries to . .
IBBS & TILLETT LTD.
124 WIGMORE STREET . LONDON . W
Telephone WEL beck 2325

RUTH NYE

Circa 1970

Ross leading a group of riders through the mews circa 1971.

Photo shoot for a magazine circa 1966.

Ruth Nye, Australian pianist now making herself well-known in London, is not too confident about horses, but she's trying hard . . . specially now that she and her husband have bought a riding school in the lovely English countryside, near Guildford, in Surrey.

Circa 1966

After one of Arrau's performances circa 1970.

Publicity photo circa 1975.

Playing Clara Schumann's piano in Braunschweig circa 2006.

Master class in Amsterdam circa 2008

Ruth and Ross with the grand children circa 2005

ACKNOWLEDGEMENTS

My thanks, first and foremost, to Terry Lewis, without whose support, assistance, intriguing conversations over long lunches, and input, this work would never have been accomplished. I thank him for the interview he did with Paolo Fazioli, and for all the CDs, DVDs, and photos with which he has kept me supplied, as well as the contacts he has facilitated for me. He is a dear and much appreciated friend, and I even need to thank him for looking after my luggage on so many occasions!

To Ruth Nye herself, who has been patient, cooperative and helpful, I offer heartfelt thanks and appreciation. She has supplied me with all information I have needed, (even if it did take a very long time to persuade her that she was worth writing about!) Once Ruth became convinced of the necessity and value of this work she engaged with full enthusiasm. She has answered so many questions, made so many corrections, and given me so much of herself without which I could never have succeeded in this project.

To Ross Nye, I am indebted for his generous warmth and hospitality on so many visits, for his encouragement of my efforts and for his good sense and good humour.

"Happy Days", dear Ruthie and Ross.

A special thanks of course needs to be given to all those wonderful and gifted pupils of Ruth's, who tolerated my presence in innumerable lessons over the years and who gave me so much inspiration and joy. I have a special love for you all.

To my daughters, Deborah Tresise and Jackie Randles, I give very special thanks for their support and assistance with typing, reading, copying and editing and photo handling. I could not have managed without either.

This work is not a scholarly treatise so I have considered it inappropriate to add a formal bibliography. However I do acknowledge a certain amount of information has been gained by my readings from the following sources:

Conversations With Arrau by Joseph Horowitz, Collins, London 1982

Everything is Connected by Daniel Barenboim, Weidenfeld and Nicolson, Orion Publishing Group, London, WC2H 9EA, 2008

The Yehudi Menuhin Catalogue and Newsletters (various years).

Various newspaper articles and clippings from many countries dug out of old trunks in the attic at Longfrey and long forgotten.

Various BBC radio programmes.

Photography is acknowledged with thanks as follows :

Recent photo of Ruth at Piano; Ruth and Ross with 4 grandchildren; and Ross and his dog:

Hugo Burnand

Ruth with Prince Charles and signing the register for her FRCM, Chris Christodoulou

Ruth with 'Dollar Prince': Fred Warren, Ruth, Australian Television Logie Winner: Vic John, All other photos have been taken by myself and by other friends, or have come from the family archives and their source no longer known.

And finally...

To all those who contributed information and valuable tributes, I give my enormous gratitude. I also offer my apologies to those whose contributions were not included.

Thanks too go to Lou Wasser, Dr Ian Baird and Stefanie Rumpelt-Meyn for their invaluable assistance with the editing, proofreading and cover design of this manuscript.

ABOUT THE AUTHOR

Roma Randles has many interests, including eleven grandchildren, and lives in Melbourne. She loves travel and, as Director of LINGUA MUSICA for over twenty years, has organised and run very successful European Music and Art tours.